Praise for *The Art of Retirement*

"As a CERTIFIED FINANCIAL PLANNER™ practitioner, I have read many financial planning books for individuals over the past 20 years. Unfortunately, most are either too light on important data or too analytical and complex for most nonprofessional readers. In *The Art of Retirement,* Gary not only addresses the important elements of retirement planning, but he does so in clear and entertaining manner. This is definitely a book that I will recommend my clients read!"

—Brad Levin, CFP®, AIF®
President and Founder, Legacy Wealth Partners

"Most books on retirement focus only on planning financially for the event. *The Art of Retirement* illustrates how retirement isn't just about how you will live your life *years* from now, but how you live your life *now*, as you build your legacy. Gary Williams' book is both inspiring and informative."

—Brad Pollard
Vice President of Information Technology, Sourcefire, Inc.

"Gary Williams has successfully tackled a daunting task in his book *The Art of Retirement*. In an easy-to-understand way, he addresses the significant financial issues many of us will face as we go through life into retirement and equally important, how to enjoy the quality of life that truly counts. It is both as simple as anyone could ask for, and through many cross-references, as sophisticated as anyone could want. This is a terrific resource told in a very reader-friendly, yet powerful, storytelling way!"

—Colin Brown
President and CEO, JM Family Enterprises, Inc.

"I have read many good books on investing, and I have read many good books on the psychology of achieving personal happiness in life, but I have never before read a book that marries these two topics together as brilliantly as Gary Williams does in *The Art of Retirement*. Creating personal wealth is a paradox in that it does not in itself create happiness, but when combined with personal wisdom, wealth can create a brilliant life full of joy, value, and love. In *The Art of Retirement*, Gary Williams weaves together a tapestry of knowledge, wisdom, experience, and guidance that will allow the reader to create an investment strategy that will lead to not only wealth, but more importantly to true happiness."

—R. Daniel Richardson, CFP®
President, Pantheon Real Estate Services

"This book artfully combines many aspects of planning for your future. Gary does a wonderful job bringing together, and making sense of, the many components that will create your retirement plan: discovering what you want out of retirement, understanding investment concepts, and developing a plan to get there."

—David Weaver, CFA
President and Portfolio Manager,
The Adams Express Company

"Where you stand is a function of where you sit. Do you know where you stand on your readiness for retirement? Sit, read, and learn where you stand. A must-read for anyone contemplating retirement."

—J.P. Bolduc
Chairman and CEO, JPB Partners

"*The Art of Retirement* gives you more than a blueprint for creating a portfolio masterpiece. Gary Williams wrote the book for anyone who wants to build a legacy of responsibility and independence."

—Jim Munchbach
Professor of Personal Finance, Bauer College of Business,
University of Houston

"Gary has absolutely nailed it in his book, *The Art of Retirement*. I loved the stories, analogies, and sage wisdom and felt challenged to refresh my own retirement strategies. If you read this book you will be more prepared both financially and emotionally for your best retirement."

—John Ledford, CFP®
President, Ledford Financial
Best-Selling Author of *Win* and *The Only Business Book You Will Ever Need*

"Gary Williams has painted a masterpiece with *The Art of Retirement*— an exceptionally well-written and easy-to-comprehend balance of investment advice, emotional guidance, and life planning. A must-read for understanding the essential issues to focus on in order to ensure a successful and gratifying retirement."

—Wayne Bloom
CEO, Commonwealth Financial Network

"Gary Williams provides a wealth of practical information on retirement, ranging from advice on preparing a nonfinancial legacy of personal values, to examining technical matters, such as investment strategies. I recommend *The Art of Retirement* for anyone interested in understanding the scope of services offered by a competent wealth manager."

—Guy Maseritz, Esq.
Business Attorney

"Books on investing are, like leadership books, often written from the perspective of a single individual and that person's idiosyncratic point of view. In *The Art of Retirement*, Gary Williams steps back and asks the reader to think more broadly about his or her life, and how retirement and one's financial goals fit into a larger whole. He then takes that broader perspective and walks you through an analytical framework that makes sense and clarifies what can often be a confusing set of choices."

—John K. Hoey
President and CEO, Y of Central Maryland

"This is a wonderful book, and so much more than a typical financial planning book. Gary's initial topic of focusing on the role of money in determining one's happiness is extremely thought provoking for anyone trying to balance being a good parent while providing one's family with financial security. The book then asks the reader to think of retirement in a holistic manner considering many things, including finances, time management, and the importance of one's legacy. Lastly the book is able to explain, in a simple and effective manner, a wide selection of technical financial planning theories. Gary's personal experience will force you to reevaluate your understanding not only of money but what is true success. Gary's professional experience is demonstrated in the wide breadth of topics that are discussed, and it is a truly insightful book that will provide you with a roadmap to achieve a successful retirement."

—Matthew K. Buckley, CPA
Board Member, Private Equity CFO Association

"Gary brings a fresh perspective to *The Art of Retirement*. He's written a tremendous resource that is a must-read for every professional in America."

—Jonathan Oleisky
President/Partner, Kalix Communications, LLC

"Gary Williams takes the challenging subject of financial planning and creates a thought-provoking, easy-to-understand, and incredibly enjoyable reading experience. This is a book that would live as comfortably in the motivational section of a bookstore as the business section. Gary's unique anecdotes, based on his family's experiences, help us understand how to find both financial security and personal happiness. For anyone who believes financial planning is daunting, this book will take them on a rewarding journey through the process of creating a financial legacy. With a smile."

—Carrie Bertuccio
Chief Operating Officer, Claar Advisors LLC

"*The Art of Retirement* is a must-read for anyone over 40! As a 30-year veteran in the industry, I will put to use many of the principles immediately."

—Jon Sundt
President and CEO, Altegris Investments

"I highly recommend this book as an enjoyable journey in understanding *The Art of Retirement,* written by a passionate financial services industry expert. The connections between Michelangelo and Gary's personal experience provide a comprehensive review of the investment process in an easy-to-follow format that can be valuable at all stages of an individual's financial life, from beginner to expert. We will utilize Gary's book for our corporate retirement planning course to help guide employees seeking a successful investment plan."

—James Gibeaut, CPA
Controller, Enterprise Holdings

"I never thought living with ALS would be part of my retirement. I have learned there is an art to life, as well as an art to retirement. Gary has mastered both!"

—Augie Nieto
Chief Inspirational Officer, Augie's Quest
Co-founder and former president of Life Fitness
Chairman, Octane Fitness

The Art of Retirement

by

GARY S. WILLIAMS, CFP®

Emerson

Front Cover Photo: Statue of Michelangelo in Florence

Dedication

This book is dedicated to those who have lost their lives to ALS. In memory of Eric Scoggins and Bruce Anderson—you will not be forgotten.

To those living with ALS—it is my hope that the revenue from the book helps to assist in funding research and finding a cure.

To O.J. Brigance and Augie Nieto—my inspiration for writing this book.

Contents

Foreword
by Ronnie Lott

"How is greatness achieved in life?" Maybe it is defined by the achievements in your occupation or by building a successful business. Perhaps it is defined by a marriage that has flourished for many years or by watching your children become valuable members of society. Or maybe it is based on how wealthy you are, or possibly how you have devoted your time or

Ronnie Lott

wealth to a worthwhile charitable cause. I can't answer this question for you—only you can answer it for yourself. However, what I can tell you is that life is more than defining moments; it is about living a life that is defining.

My football career has defined me personally, as well as from the public's perspective, for most of my adult life. From my early days, while attending Eisenhower High School to leading the University of Southern California Trojans to a national championship in 1978 and playing in two Rose Bowls, the game of football provided me with a sense of accomplishment and recognition. I was blessed to continue my football career after college, when I was selected in the first round of the 1981 NFL draft. After 14 professional seasons that included four Super Bowl rings and 10 Pro Bowls, I was elected to the Hall of Fame in 2000.

This honor solidified my career, and it gratified me to know my football career culminated on what many consider to be the highest note.

I always knew the time would come when I would close that chapter of my life; I would not be able to play football forever. Fortunately, I was able to transition to my post-football career through various business ventures and running my foundation, All Stars Helping Kids. While my business endeavors and philanthropic work do not give me the same level of exhilaration as did 50,000 fans cheering after an interception or a touchdown-saving tackle, they provide me with a different type of appreciation. You see, it is not about *what you are doing* that can bring you happiness; it is about *how you do what you are doing*. If you are passionate about something and work hard toward your vision, greatness can be achieved.

Achieving greatness in the game of football required intense fortitude, focus, dedication, and, literally, blood, sweat, and sometimes tears. Even though your career or time spent raising a family may not be as constantly intense as playing football, it is similar in a sense. Like me, you dedicate your time and energy to doing something that brings you the possibility of recognition (good and bad), a pat on the back, a "congratulations," or just a feeling of achievement. I believe everyone wants to feel appreciated for a job well done. This sense of purpose can come from whatever you are passionate about—your career, giving back to the community, spending time with your family and friends, or faith-based volunteer activities.

As you think about how *you* will achieve greatness, my suggestion is to "exhaust life." Figure out what you are passionate about and exhaust your life around it. In other words, don't just sit on the sideline and watch life; instead, truly and fervently live it.

The great thing about life is, just like this book, once one chapter ends, another one begins. Exhaust each chapter of your life. If you do this, your life's story will be, as Gary calls it . . . "a masterpiece."

—Ronnie Lott
Former NFL Player, NFL Hall of Famer,
and founder of All Stars Helping Kids Foundation

Preface

THE DEFINITION OF *RETIREMENT* MEANS DIFFERENT THINGS TO DIFFERENT people. That said, retirement planning can have many different meanings. The definition can focus on finances or lifestyle and can include many variables, such as location, activities, and health care, depending on your individual situation. It is the uniqueness of retirement that makes retirement planning much different and more difficult than planning for other goals in life.

This book will serve as a general guide, helping you to understand retirement planning from many perspectives. It is divided into two parts. In Part I, Creating Your Masterpiece, we delve into such topics as money (how it relates to happiness), sources of financial information, lifestyle and life during retirement, and leaving a legacy, and conclude with a discussion on financial planning. In Part II, The Art of Investing, we discuss concepts such as risk and diversification, unique investment strategies to consider for your portfolio, and determining when and how to find a financial advisor (if you believe you need professional advice).

When I entered the business of financial planning in 1994, investing seemed easier. Traditional investments, such as publicly traded stocks and bonds were the prevalent investment strategies in the 1990s. Further, time-tested strategies and concepts, such as dollar-cost averaging, investing regularly, and asset allocation, seemed to be what were needed to invest wisely and reach your financial goals.

A lot has changed over the past 19 years, and I am sure a lot will change over the next 19. Knowing that change is inevitable is not the difficult part of life; it is learning to adapt to these changes that can sometimes prove challenging. Life has become more complex—from the number and types of investments, to the personal and economic impact of recessions and other crisis events around the globe. Trying to discern who to trust and listen to, due to the vast amount of information available, has become overwhelming. Everything—from massive fraud, stock bubbles, financial meltdowns, natural disasters, and terrorism, to name a few—has us questioning planning, investments, and in some cases, the value of life itself.

Throughout this book, I attempt to give sound investment guidance, retirement planning considerations, and objective insight on reliable sources of information, while taking you on a journey that compares your life to a masterpiece of art. With the help of Michelangelo's life and art, we will create a masterpiece—a rich and rewarding life—that is centered on you.

Introduction

MICHELANGELO WAS ONE OF THE GREATEST sculptors of the Italian Renaissance and one of the world's greatest painters and architects. Against all odds—his mother died when he was six, his impoverished father considered his son's desire to become an artist unworthy of the family name—he relentlessly pursued his artistic passions. In 1505 he was commissioned to paint the ceiling of the Sistine Chapel, which took five years, and meanwhile he continued sculpting, architecture, and writing poetry. He was a man for all

Michelangelo di Lodovico Buonarroti Simoni (1475–1564)

seasons, and he probably never heard the word *retirement*. He was actually sculpting the *Rondanini Pietà* when he became ill and died in 1564 at age 89.

What do Michelangelo and his life have to do with a book about retirement planning? Well, first let me explain just a bit: He created masterpieces, but also understood that his own life was a masterpiece and, at the same time, a work in progress. It is here that we should follow Michelangelo's example of living life to the fullest to create our own life's masterpiece. Then we can create our plan, follow our passions, and continue to enjoy happiness and success well into retirement.

We all know that Michelangelo was a genius. The original "Renaissance man," he was generally acknowledged to have been one of the few people to create masterpieces in three separate fields (sculpture, painting, and architecture). How did Michelangelo move among these fields with such outstanding success, achieving mastery in each one? He was encouraged and recognized, and he was immersed in his love for each of his masterpieces. His inner drive led him to greatness; he let nothing get in his way. These elements are what you need to build your own extraordinary career and life.

Michelangelo maintained his incredible lifestyle well into his "golden years," which kept him alive until he was 89 years old—well beyond the longevity for men and women of that century. His life begs the question: What will *you* be doing in *your* golden years?

PART ONE

Creating Your Masterpiece

1 | Perspective Matters

"You are the masterpiece of your own life. You are the Michelangelo of your own life. The David you are sculpturing is you."

—Rhonda Byrne, *The Secret*

BEFORE WE DELVE INTO A TRADITIONAL DISCUSSION ON RETIREMENT planning and investments, you need to understand what money means to you and where it fits into your value system. You see, figuring out how much money you need to save and where you need to invest it is the easy part of retirement planning.

Conversely, appreciating your values and your value system (and if you have a spouse or partner, that person's value system as it relates to money, since it might be different from yours) requires some introspective thought. It requires us to look at our life and determine what is important to us and why. Many important nonfinancial questions need to be answered prior to determining how you should invest and save. Some examples include:

- In today's world of too much information and not nearly enough wisdom, how do you distinguish among your resources for advice and guidance? (Chapter 2)
- What are you going to do, day in and day out, during "retirement"? You likely have been focused on a routine of working 40-plus hours a week. If you are no longer working those hours, how are you going to find a meaningful way to spend your time? (Chapter 3)

- How do you want to be remembered by your family and friends? What kind of legacy do you want to leave financially and, even more importantly, nonfinancially? (Chapter 4)
- What does financial planning mean, and how do you determine whether it is appropriate for you? (Chapter 5)

No need to worry. We are going to help you answer all these questions and more!

HOW DO THE ROSES SMELL?

Our perspective, or the way we view life, is influenced by our experiences and is instrumental in determining how and why we make the decisions we do. Gaining an understanding of what is truly important to us—our values—will be a critical step in planning for our futures.

Behaviorists believe that our environment is a determining factor in the human condition and in shaping who we are, which means the experiences we encounter in our life, beginning when we take our first breath, help shape our future years. Life is truly an "artwork in progress." Unfortunately, you will not know what your completed masterpiece looks like, but your family and friends will as they reflect back on their experiences with you. Your legacy and how you are remembered are part of the masterpiece.

As we try to gain perspective of our values and how we feel about money, we need to consider what makes us happy. Day to day, most of us don't consciously think to ourselves, "Am I happy?" We get to a point in life where we hit a plateau, a level of happiness where we are content. Our life is going along like a freight train that is trying to get to its next destination.

> **Key Point:** *Take time to "smell the roses." You can't begin to plan for your future (i.e., retirement) until you know where you have been. And you won't know where you have been unless you truly experienced it and didn't let it pass you by.*

We are the mindless victims of a culture that emphasizes material prosperity (big house, fancy car, attractive looks, prestige, etc.) as the definition of happiness.

ADVERSITY IS PART OF LIFE

Our lives have a number of things in common. One of them is that we will all deal with adversity at some point. It could be financial, such as the stock market wiping out part of our portfolio or a business failing. Or it could possibly be a disease in ourselves, a family member, or a friend. It is this adversity that helps us gain perspective and reminds us what truly matters in life. For example, financial struggles and challenges experienced early in our lives can be viewed as hindrances and obstacles, or they can challenge us to overcome deficiencies.

The purpose of this chapter is not to determine the characteristics you need in order to become the type of individual who looks at problems in life and says, "The glass is half full," rather than one who says, "Woe is me." I want you to understand and appreciate that life will sometimes hit you with an unexpected setback, but you can learn from it and become a better person because of it. In essence, I believe the environment can challenge and inspire you, or it can defeat you. It's what you do with the challenges that delivers the eventual outcome.

Key Point: *Setbacks will happen. You cannot control certain things in life. Focus on what you can control.*

We can only challenge ourselves to try our hardest at everything we attempt in life. As most parents would, I tell my kids as they study for a test or take the field for a sports competition, "Try your best and have fun." I think this is the way we should look at life. So, when the stock market corrects (and it will periodically) and your investment value decreases, remind yourself that you are still blessed with life, and you still have family and friends—the most important things in life—who care about you.

O.J. and Chanda Brigance

O.J. BRIGANCE . . .

One of the reasons I am writing this book is to raise money for research to help find a cure for amyotrophic lateral sclerosis (ALS), also known as Lou Gehrig's disease. Finding a cure is near and dear to my heart. My father-in-law, Bruce Anderson, passed away from this dreadful disease, and currently my friend, O.J. Brigance, is battling ALS. O.J. is someone who inspires me, but more importantly, gives me perspective.

. . . is a champion.

O.J. Brigance was a championship football player in the Canadian Football League (CFL) and the National Football League (NFL).

He played his college football at Rice University. When he reached his senior year in college, he approached his head coach about playing professionally. The advice he received: "Take the degree and enter the business world." O.J. was motivated by the fact that many believed he was incapable of playing at the next level. O.J. thanked his coach for the advice and pursued playing professional football.

When asked questions about his life, O.J. gave answers that provide perspective and inspiration. It is important to understand that O.J. can't speak with his own voice due to ALS. Through the use of a sophisticated communication device, he uses his eyes to focus on letters and words that that are on a computer screen. The device then speaks the words that he has typed with his eyes! When asked about his motivation and the discipline needed to go from an undrafted free agent to a 12-year professional player, O.J. responded, "Money was never a motivation, but a benefit of pursuing my God-given dream." He went on to say, "I was fortunate to never work a day in my life because I had been blessed to do what I love to do."

He began his pro career in the CFL, with the B.C. Lions in 1991. He played three years and 54 games with the Lions, his best season being 1993 when he recorded 20 sacks and was an All-Star. He played his next two seasons with the Baltimore Stallions, where he was an All-Pro in 1995, recording 7 sacks and helping win the Grey Cup championship.

The NFL called in 1996, and O.J. began a seven-year career. He played four seasons and 60 games with the Miami Dolphins before joining the Baltimore Ravens in 2000. He played 16 games for the Ravens and won a Super Bowl ring. He played 2001 and 2002 with the St. Louis Rams (21 games) and finished his career with the New England Patriots in 2002. Throughout his NFL career, he was primarily a special teams player. In total, he played 12 years as a professional football player.

He is one of the few players who won both a CFL and NFL championship. And he is the only one to accomplish this feat in the same city, Baltimore (Stallions and Ravens).

In Miami, Brigance was involved in a number of community organizations, including Habitat for Humanity, Cystic Fibrosis Foundation, and the Daily Food Bank. Brigance was honored with the NFL Players Association's Unsung Hero award in 1999.

In 2007, at age 38, O.J. was diagnosed with ALS, a motor neuron disease, and given a life expectancy of three to five years. His disease has progressed and he now requires machines and people to help him with every task that most people take for granted, such as breathing, eating, bathing, dressing, and talking. He can move only his eyes and when he sees you, he "smiles" with his eyes. Even though he can't move his body, his mind still works and is sharper than ever. He still enthusiastically goes to work every day as the Senior Advisor to Player Development for the Baltimore Ravens.

. . . gives me perspective.

What gives O.J. his upbeat perspective? Here is a man battling a fatal disease with tenacity, not letting it defeat him. With his wife, Chanda, O.J. is putting tremendous effort into the Brigance Brigade Foundation in order to raise funds to improve the quality of life for other ALS patients and their families by providing access to vital treatment, equipment, and support services. The Brigance Brigade Foundation also partners with the Robert Packard Center for ALS Research at Johns Hopkins and supports the critical funding of research for a cure. When I asked him about his perspective and his desire to make our world a better place, his response was the following:

"To whom much is given, much is expected." Over my life I have come to learn that the most valuable things have no price tag on them. Love, joy, peace, and health to name a few. We are all conduits to give because we have been given. If we approach life with a closed-fist mentality, true, nothing will get away from us, but nothing will be able to enter our hands either. We are put on the earth to serve others in some capacity.

How does O.J. stay focused on life and the "bigger picture"? What kind of lens is necessary to have this selflessness and courage when being challenged in the way that O.J. is being challenged? As O.J. puts it:

Each stage in life serves as a stepping stone for the next. There are never mistakes in life, but learning opportunities. As we go through life's adversities they are strengthening us for new triumphs and challenges to come. Our faith in Jesus Christ has allowed my wife Chanda and me to keep a singular focus, no matter what comes our way. One of my favorite sayings is, "Life is a lot like school, there is never promotion without testing."

When I first met O.J., I knew we would become friends. In his office at the Baltimore Ravens "Castle," he has financial magazines fanned out on his coffee table. In addition to our common passion to find a cure for ALS, we share a passion for helping others make smart financial

> **Key Point:** *Keep your perspective; it could always be worse. Be grateful for your blessings in life.*

decisions. As part of O.J.'s position with the Baltimore Ravens, he counsels players about finances. Beyond a perspective on life, O.J. gives a perspective on money. As O.J. puts it:

> *Perspective is defined as a particular evaluation of a situation or facts, especially from one person's point of view. A person can have little financial means and still have every provision met. We can't get caught up comparing ourselves to what others have around us, but be grateful for whatever capacity one does have. I don't mean settling, but contentment in your current situation until your time of promotion comes. I have learned appreciation for physical and mental health and peace of mind.*

He goes on to say:

> *My experiences and life perspective have definitely influenced my perspective on money. While money is very necessary to live, the amount of money is never the determinant of a person's self-worth or happiness. No amount of money can cure me of ALS at the moment, but my attitude in the midst of this trial will determine how I continue to live and impact the world around me. I was given a quote that says, "Everyone is suffering, but misery is optional." The one thing we can always control is our attitude.*

. . . and inspires me every day.

I run four or five times a week for exercise. My typical course is about five miles through Patapsco State Park on the "blue trail." The blue trail is mostly flat, but parts of it are steep and require me to find an inner drive in order to get up those hills. One part in particular is extremely rugged and steep, and it is there that I think of O.J. and ask myself, "If O.J. had a chance to do this, would he give up?" I get to the top, every time, without stopping. After we find a cure for ALS, I am going to take O.J. to the blue trail and run it with him! We all need someone to inspire us—for me, that person is O.J. Brigance.

O.J. gives me perspective. Hopefully his thoughts resonate well with you, too.

SELF-ACTUALIZATION

Just as Michelangelo did, everyone creates his or her own "masterpiece," but happiness in life can sometimes feel like an impossible task. We need to remember that happiness is a state of mind and a state of being. It is our value system, the way we look at things, people, and situations that can help make us happy. Happiness is also about having gratitude for the abundance we have in our lives. This state of mind usually leads to our success in life, in our work, and with our families.

According to an international study on happiness conducted by the *New Scientist* international magazine, research within western culture suggests that once our basic needs for security, safety, and health

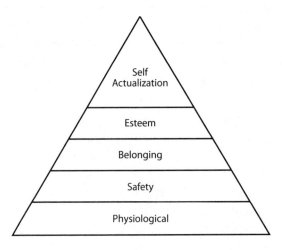

Self Actualization

Esteem

Belonging

Safety

Physiological

are met, our happiness and quality of life are affected most significantly
by the quality of our personal relationships with ourselves, our partner,
family, friends, and community. Abraham Maslow, the world-renowned
professor of psychology famous for developing a step-ladder theory of
happiness and motivation (Maslow's Hierarchy of Needs), confirmed
that once fundamental human needs are met then one can progress to
the satisfaction of higher needs, and on up the hierarchical ladder to
increasing happiness. Being happy will, among many things, make you
a better spouse, better father or mother, and better employee, which
should help your income grow and provide peace of mind about maintaining your current lifestyle as well as having a comfortable retirement.
Shawn Achor, founder of Good Think, Inc., author of "The Happiness Advantage," and graduate of Harvard University, magna cum laude
draws the same conclusion. He suggests that we should put happiness
first in order to become more successful and have a fulfilled life, and
not the other way around (i.e., a job promotion will lead to happiness).

According to Kol Birke, financial behavior specialist at Commonwealth Financial Network, "Positive emotions are actually the fuel
that drives us forward, and they trigger areas of the brain that allow
us to think more creatively and literally
see more options. While negative emotions are there to help us react quickly to
danger, positive emotions are there to help
ensure our actions are the right ones."

> **Key Point:** *Happiness breeds happiness. Don't wait until you retire or get the next promotion or build your portfolio to "x." If you are happy with what you do have, you will be a success.*

MY PURSUIT OF HAPPINESS

Like many, I have experienced adversity
and challenges in my life. I have also experienced more success than I ever imagined.
I would like to share with you a brief story about my upbringing,
what I learned, and how my experiences and my environment affected
my perspective. Along the way I came to realize that wealthy people
are not always happy, and that poor or underprivileged people are not
always unhappy. So, let me tell you the story of my father and mother,

and you may come to see that from early childhood my understanding, appreciation, and perspective began to surface.

My father was a bricklayer in the coke ovens at Bethlehem Steel Corporation. The life of a steelworker was hard. The 1980s were a tough time for an old-line industry: It faced serious environmental problems with high price tags for fixing them, intense competition from overseas, rapidly changing markets, severe labor problems, and new technologies too costly to put in place. In the early 1980s, the U.S. steel industry went from world dominance to about 10 percent of the market, with Japan taking over as leader. It was tough for my father.

My mom was a homemaker who passed away from colon cancer when I was eight years old. I watched my father go through numerous layoffs and furloughs, and for many years of my childhood we relied on food stamps and unemployment insurance due to the depressed steel industry.

We knew good times, too. My father was fortunate to also work as a bread-delivery truck driver for a number of years, which certainly went a long way toward paying our bills. Needless to say, my father did not have an investment portfolio. He lived, like many, from paycheck to paycheck. I remember getting $10 from the ATM machine at Maryland National Bank and the balance on the receipt was $500. I was still young, probably around 10 years old, but I remember thinking to myself, "This is not a lot of money." I worried. But although I knew my father had a cash reserve of only $500, we had a house, food, one working burner on the stovetop, and heat.

In many ways at that time, I was also fortunate. You see, a few months before my mother died she made sure that we lived in a location that would give me and my brother that opportunity to succeed. Our home on Silver Creek Road was purchased by the federal government be-cause it was in a flood plain. My mother wanted to make sure the "nest" was well-made when she left this world, so she made a point of finding a house in a nice neighborhood. I believe this task—to make sure we got into another home—was one of the things that kept her alive.

We moved on April 1, 1979. My mother died just 16 days later, on April 17. It was a defining moment for me. Our new home was in suburban Baltimore County, Maryland. It was this new setting that allowed me to get a good public education and, at the same time, witness a socioeconomic setting that allowed me to appreciate different levels of success. This distinction was important to me because I had witnessed my hard-working father's struggle when I was younger, and although I didn't know it at the time, I was building up a force inside me that was going to help me do whatever it took to avoid those financial struggles for my future family.

"Wait a minute," you say! *"I thought this was a book about retirement planning. What is going on here? This sounds like one of those feel-good stories about how someone made something of his life."* Well, the answer is, it's just a small part of the overall message of the book that I use to illustrate the concept of how your plan for retirement is shaped from your experiences in life, including your early years. Numerous studies support the premise that the environment in which we grow up and live plays a crucial part in our future success and happiness. One of those studies was the World Values Survey. In 2003, the survey[1] looked at people in 65 nations [and regions] and found that the world's happiest countries with the most satisfied people are Puerto Rico and Mexico, and those with the most optimistic people are Nigeria and Mexico. The United States was sixteenth on the list. To help you appreciate these statistics, you need to understand a few important points:

- In 2003, material prosperity, measured by a nation's gross domestic product (GDP) per capita was $37,800 in the United States. Puerto Rico was $16,800, Mexico was $9,000, and Nigeria was $800.
- At the time, Puerto Rico suffered from a high murder rate and double-digit unemployment.
- Nigeria was one of the world's most corrupt countries, government service and infrastructure was unreliable, and violence was widespread.
- Nigeria was ranked 152nd out of 175 countries (24th from bottom) for life expectancy, health, education, standard of living, and literacy.

---

[1] *http://www.worldvaluessurvey.org*

Interestingly, studies have shown that the norm in our society is pursuit of financial goals only to find that when we reach them we are no happier. Clive Hamilton of the Australia Institute found in a national survey that high-income earners actually feel less satisfied and prosperous than low-income earners! While 9 percent of the

> **Key Point:** *Happiness is not just about how much money is in your portfolio or how many material possessions you own.*

lowest income earners (less than $25,000 per year) were happy with what they earned and 21 percent reported being totally satisfied with life, only 5 percent of the highest income earners (more than $100,000 per year) felt prosperous, and just 13 percent were totally satisfied with life generally. This outcome seems counterintuitive. But similarly, according to U.S. statistics, happiness of wealthy people is only slightly better than average, with income above $20,000 per capita yielding, at best, minimal increases in happiness. Further, studies show that people who value money highly tend to be less happy than those who place the highest priority on love and relationships. Having enough for a basic standard of living IS important, but once we have enough to live on, the biggest happiness gains are reaped from the quality of our human relationships.

Now, for the record, I have to admit something: I *used* to think money was everything. After graduating from college, I had money on my mind and I wanted to make lots of it! I entered the financial services industry right out of college and was hired by IDS (Investors Diversified Services), a subsidiary of American Express. After a few years of cold calling and building my practice, I decided to take a job in management and leadership in San Antonio, Texas, with American Express Financial Advisors. I realized early into that position I didn't enjoy my management job and that "money is not everything." I decided to go back to what I then realized was my true calling and passion—working with individual clients and financial planning that helps them understand money, how it can work for them, and the importance of having sufficient assets to retire comfortably.

That being said, the main point of this chapter on perspective is for you to appreciate that everyone is different, and your surroundings and environment determine your attitude toward money and your values regarding money. Although adversity during your younger years may help you appreciate your successes later in life, it can also help you to realize that money is a means to an end. As we move forward in our discussion, remind yourself that retirement planning is more than how much is in your portfolio. Last, remember, your life is comparable to a great work of art; it is your own masterpiece.

PERSPECTIVE HELPED MICHELANGELO, TOO

The original idea from the papal commission was to have Michelangelo paint 12 apostles on the ceiling of the Sistine Chapel, but once he was up on the ceiling that idea did not work for him. After spending time examining the 68-foot-high, 12,000-square-foot ceiling, he gained perspective. He realized that, after studying the shape and size of the ceiling, he needed to do something quite different. He and his assistants stretched taut strings across the entire length and width of the chapel and then proceeded to chalk lines against the prepared surface. This provided a linear framework for the entire ceiling. He used this planning to create 175 distinct picture vaults. He did all of this before even picking up a brush.

Ultimately, he created the masterpiece that is one of the most-visited tourist destinations—some 5 million visitors a year. He designed a fresco of the stories of Genesis, fanning out from the center with the "Creation of Adam" that shows God reaching down from heaven and touching the finger of Adam, along with images of biblical prophets and ancestors of Jesus. Today, as I am writing this book, the ceiling of the Sistine Chapel, one of the world's most iconic pieces of art, celebrates its 500th anniversary; it has truly brought joy and amazement to those who have seen it.

Like Michelangelo, sometimes we need perspective to create *our masterpiece.*

"Ancora imparo." [translated: *"I am still learning."*]
—**Michelangelo (at age 87)**

2 | Choose Your Colors Carefully—Then Achieve the Right Mixture

"A man paints with his brains and not with his hands."

—Michelangelo

IN CHAPTER 1, WE DISCUSSED THE REALIZATION THAT LIFE MAY DEAL us setbacks and adversity that we will need to accept and overcome; investments may not pan out, our health may create challenges, or we may not have been able to save as much as we would have hoped for retirement. However, with perspective we are better able to appreciate *what we do have* and make the most of it.

We learned that our general level of happiness along with our experiences in life help us define our attitudes and values as they relate to money. One of the main points from Chapter 1 was to remind us of the well-known saying, "Money can't buy happiness." But it can buy security, peace of mind, and the means to do the things we want to do in retirement.

From the beginning of our working years, we need to be diligent in managing our money, making sure we make the right decisions in preserving and protecting our assets. It's important to stay informed, and with today's abundance of information on TV, radio, magazines, newspapers, how-to books, and the Internet 24 hours a day, seven days a week, you'll never be without "expert" sources. However, like Michelangelo, you need to be discriminating in your choices because the result may be either a masterpiece or complete chaos and disappointment. Michelangelo had a vast array of colors and pigments from which to choose, but the key to a masterpiece is finding the *right mixture* of these colors.

Colors can have a positive or negative impact on a person admiring a painting; colors can stir emotions and create moods. With a painting, after an artist mixes the right combination of colors and then applies them to her canvas, she will soon know whether she has actually created a masterpiece. Similarly, investments, and more specifically their performance, can stir emotions and sometimes influence your decision-making ability. Investment vehicles in your portfolio sometimes won't work out as planned, just as colors on a painting can clash if you don't choose them with critical care and skill. Said differently, creating a perfect balance with colors will add maximum impact to a work of art, just as carefully selected investments should create the appropriate "balance" for your portfolio.

Michelangelo listened carefully to his mentor, the Italian sculptor Bertoldo di Giovanni, who was the head teacher of the School for Painters and Sculptors in Florence. He didn't take advice from lesser teachers. Investment advice is similar. Relying on the right *sources* of information, in the right amounts, will give you the information needed to make smart decisions with your money. This chapter focuses on how to make the best choices by cutting through the financial "noise," and determining who to listen to (or choose to work with) when it concerns the growth, preservation, and protection of your money.

INFORMATION, BEHAVIORS, AND FADS

Sometimes figuring out who to turn to for guidance on financial matters can be confusing. Partly because of the messages we receive from the media and partly because you, as a human being, are subject to your emotions and societal pressure. We will focus on three specific causes of this confusion: the abundance of information, our behaviors regarding money, and dealing with fads.

SIFTING THROUGH THE INFORMATION OVERLOAD

Our information-based society is often plagued with excess, particularly in connection with advice about money and investing. In addition to the media clatter, it is my opinion that financial "entertainers" like Suze Orman, Jim Cramer, and others often add to the confusion of overwhelming choices. Fidelity wants us to follow a green path. Charles Schwab wants us to talk with Chuck. And my favorite of all, "when EF Hutton talks, people listen." Sometimes it is difficult to know where to go for help. Although general advice may be appropriate for the masses, everyone's situation is different and it becomes difficult to determine who to listen to. Just like a snowflake or work of art, each individual is different.

> **Key Point:** *Even though some mass-publicized advice is general and appropriate for the millions of viewers who may be watching the "financial" show, it may not be appropriate for your situation.*

Information overload results from two main factors:

One is pure quantity. Perhaps some people like having a lot of choices, and it might be liberating to some extent. But as Kol Birke mentions in his article, "Exploring Behavioral Finance," published in the *Commonwealth Business Review*, "If people have too many choices, they may be unable to make a decision at all." This situation is called the "paradox of choice." Consequently, after reviewing all the options, you become dissatisfied with whatever decision you choose. It is quite the dilemma, especially for investors. Hence, understanding the basics of behavioral finance can be helpful for most people.

The second factor is option similarity. If everything seems the same, differentiating one alternative from another is confusing and difficult.

Various academic studies have also shown that information overload can lead to bad decisions and passivity. For example, research[2] on this issue by Julie Agnew and Lisa Szykman (both professors at the Mason School of Business, College of William and Mary), published in the *Journal of Behavioral Finance*, reveals that people, particularly those with a low level of financial knowledge, suffer from overload, which leads them to take the path of least resistance, and many are simply overwhelmed and cannot cope at all. But before we explore the emotional and behavioral aspects of information overload and how it may affect you, let's discuss a little history (as well as my own perspective) of this news media phenomenon.

HOW DID WE GET HERE?

From the late 1940s through most of the 1980s, we relied on the CBS, NBC, and ABC evening news shows with famous newsmen like Mike Wallace, Walter Cronkite, John Cameron Swayze and even as far back as pioneers Edward R. Murrow and Eric Sevareid! We also relied on radio and newspapers that, in some cases, were delivered up to three times each day.

We then move forward to the 1980s and 1990s with 24/7 news on cable television:[3]

- In 1980, Ted Turner founded CNN (Cable News Network) the first 24-hour news channel, which now has about 100 million viewers.
- In 1989, CNBC was launched as the Consumer News and Business Channel, now with 390 million viewers.
- In 1996, Fox News Channel (Fox News) began broadcasting and now has 85 million viewers.
- In 1996, MSNBC was launched and now has 83 million viewers.

---

[2] *http://mason.wm.edu/faculty/agnew_j/documents/assetallocation.pdf*

[3] *http://stateofthemedia.org/2012/cable-cnn-ends-its-ratings-slide-fox-falls-again/cable-by-the-numbers*

That's a staggering number of people being bombarded with news of every kind. And that includes you! News has become a 24/7 source of entertainment.

I remember back in the mid-1990s when AOL (America Online) mailed disks to my home on a weekly basis. I also saw these disks in stores, and eventually I wanted to know what they were all about. My wife and I put the disk into the computer and installed the program. After we heard the sound of the modem dialing, we were on the Internet! It was fascinating, to say the least. Of course, now we have high-speed Internet that provides us access to thousands of financial websites, including those of television networks, financial advisors, mutual fund companies, insurance companies, and blogs. The list goes on and on.

Unfortunately, most of these news media and Internet sites are for-profit businesses that sell advertising to pay the cost of hiring staff to produce material for the site or show. To successfully sell advertising, the sensationalism of markets and investments is used to stir our interest and emotions. Unfortunately, when producers choose this approach it is difficult to discern the difference between fact and fiction.

As Birke tells us, "Watching our investments rise and fall triggers the same areas of the brain as cocaine does. If we don't want to put ourselves in danger of harmful reactions, we need to focus on our longer-term goals, and possibly even shut off the infotainment." But that kind of focus is easier said than done when we are surrounded by the "noise."

IF IT IS IN *MONEY* MAGAZINE, IT MUST BE GOOD ADVICE, RIGHT?

Every year in December, CNNMoney publishes its annual "picks" for stocks to invest in for the upcoming year. Let's go back a few years and take a look at how its picks for 2008 fared. On December 14, 2007, CNNMoney published a column titled, "The best stocks for 2008: We've found ten stocks that will *thrive* despite—or even benefit from— the troubles facing the markets next year." The column mentions,

"We think the U.S. economy will slow in 2008, but narrowly miss an outright recession. We expect the overall stock market to bounce around, as it did this year [2007], and deliver anemic single-digit returns."

The average readers are saying to themselves, "This is CNNMoney, they wouldn't print it unless they are confident," right?

Unfortunately, we know how 2008 turned out. The stocks CNNMoney recommended for 2008[4] were as follows (I have added in the 2008 return after each name):

Annaly Capital, −1.27% (Source: Morningstar®)

Berkshire Hathaway, Class B, −32.14% (Source: Morningstar®)

Dick's Sporting Goods, −49.17% (Source: Morningstar®)

Electronic Arts, −72.54% (Source: Morningstar®)

Genentech, +23.6% (Source: Investor Relations Department for Roche)

General Electric, −52.95% (Source: Morningstar®)

Jacob's Engineering, −49.69% (Source: Morningstar®)

Merrill Lynch, −77.21% (Source: Investor Relations Department for Bank of America)

Petrobras, −55.60% (Source: Morningstar®)

St. Joe, −29.90% (Source: Morningstar®)

Of course, Genentech, due to a buyout by Roche, did extremely well. Also, Annaly Capital, St. Joe, and Berkshire Hathaway did better than the S&P 500 Index[5] (which lost 37% in 2008). However, they said they had stocks that would "thrive." I would not call this portfolio

---

[4] *http://money.cnn.com/2007/12/10/markets/best_stocks_2008.fortune/index.htm*

[5] The S&P 500 Index is a broad-based measurement of changes in stock market conditions based on the average performance of 500 widely held common stocks. All indices are unmanaged and investors cannot actually invest directly into an index. Unlike investments, indices do not incur management fees, charges, or expenses. Past performance does not guarantee future results.

thriving! In fact, if you had invested equally into these stocks in 2008, you would have lost 39.84 percent!

The point is, even the most respected news outlets, which typically provide broad and good general guidance, should be considered just that—broad and general guidance—and not specific investment recommendations. News outlets, for liability purposes, will state in fine print that the viewer/reader should consult with a financial, accounting or legal professional for their advice before making any decisions based on any information provided by the news outlets. Now, I consider THAT good advice.

WE NEED TO QUIET THE NOISE

So here is the scenario: It's Tuesday morning, and an investor turns on the TV and sees the market is down by 200 points. A major news network flashes a blinking red bar across the bottom of the screen: BREAKING NEWS: MARKET DOWN 200 POINTS! In the heat of panic, the investor calls his broker and expresses concern. Should the investor be concerned about this situation? Or is it simply the squawking of Chicken Little in the well-known fairy tale of the same name: "The sky is falling, the sky is falling," Chicken Little would run around warning the barnyard of impending doom. We all get a little "chicken" when fear and uncertainty obscure our thoughts. The investor's emotional bias is getting the better of him; most notably, overreaction and loss aversion. Even Peter Lynch, legendary investor and former manager and current research consultant of Fidelity Magellan mutual fund fame, refers to warnings about the sky falling as "noise."

The real question is: Is the market dropping by 200 points worthy of the title "breaking news"? I think not; in fact, it is commonplace. Since 2008, the S&P 500 has dropped by at least 1 percent during a given day nearly 200 times![6]

Major news websites tend to instigate a response by their use of bright and blinking colors and the tone of the anchors. Why would

---

[6] Commonwealth Financial Network, *www.commonwealth.com*

they use these tactics? The answer is that investors are more likely to fixate on this "market meltdown" and stay glued to their TV for a while to see what will happen next (and in the meantime, news networks are paid substantial sums of money to go to numerous commercial breaks or to "sponsored by" show segments).

The world is a complex place and has become globalized from a financial sense. What happens across the world's vast oceans directly affects our markets now. Fifty years ago, this was not necessarily the case. This complexity opens up the door for opinion. And when you give people an opportunity to share their opinions—whether through blog, podcast, television show, radio, column, or website—they will take advantage of it. I compare it to 1960s pop culture icon, Andy Warhol's expression, "15 minutes of fame," a phrase he coined in 1968. To me, it has to do with the proliferation of fame in the information age and, more recently, the democratization of media outlets brought about by the advent of the Internet. Because so many channels are available through which an individual might attain fame, virtually anyone can become famous for a brief period of time. It's something to think about while listening to the investment "gurus." Also, with the many places to post opinions, it is easy to appreciate the multitude of directions toward which investors can be pointed.

Sometimes what we see on television and read in magazines should have the following disclosure: WARNING: FOR ENTERTAINMENT PURPOSES ONLY. Remember, don't believe everything you see or read.

HOW OUR BEHAVIORS AFFECT OUR DECISIONS

The central tenet of behavioral finance is that people aren't purely rational when they make financial decisions. In addition, investors are likely to exhibit any number of specific behaviors that drive them to make all kinds of counterproductive decisions. Behavioral finance got its start in the 1970s with the publication of groundbreaking research[7]

---

[7] http://www.sjsu.edu/faculty/watkins/prospect.htm

by two psychologists, Amos Tversky and Daniel Kahneman. Their
findings focused on what they called the "prospect theory," which
contended that investors:

- Are considerably more affected by losses than by gains of the same
  size—something called "loss aversion."
- Suffer from "inertia"; people prefer to stick with the status quo.
- Worry due to the "fear of regret," which occurs when investors
  make foolish investment decisions simply because, for example,
  their friends or business associates are buying or investing in the
  same vehicles.

Additional research[8] done in the 1990s by Richard Thaler of
the University of Chicago and Shlomo Benartzi of UCLA back up
the theory; their research found several reasons why participation in
401(k) plans tended to be lower than expected. The reasons are rooted
in three key psychological principles, two of which were just mentioned: inertia and loss aversion, plus myopia (a focus on short-term
results even if the investment horizon is long) as well as plain old
procrastination.

When we combine loss aversion with myopia, we have yet another behavioral finance term: *myopic loss aversion*. Investors who check
on the value of their portfolios with great frequency may be suffering from this condition. Investors who check their portfolio daily are
more likely to abandon their well-thought-out investment allocation,
especially in bear markets when the frequency of losing days (as well as
the intensity of the losses) is greater. So, given that investors are suscep-
tible to loss aversion, and the chances of observing a loss has a higher
probability if you check your portfolio more often (i.e., check every
day versus every year, due to myopia), how often should you check the
value of your accounts?

---

[8] *http://faculty.chicagobooth.edu/richard.thaler/research/pdf/Risk-AversionOr.pdf*

The answer is "it depends." It depends on many things, including the following:

- Your capacity for self-awareness and emotional competence to understand myopic loss aversion and, therefore, avoid making poor investment decisions.

- Whether you are relying on a professional to manage your portfolio, and if your advisor is competent, you can check less often (because they are monitoring your portfolio for you).

- Whether you are using passive or actively managed funds (that would require additional monitoring).

Let's take a look at additional common psychological pitfalls that regularly affect investors. Keep in mind, though, that many of these pitfalls can be avoided if you focus on your investment time horizon (i.e., decide whether you are in for the short term or the long term). When you determine your time horizon, you probably will find that other aspects of investing become easier for you. These Top 10 pitfalls were discussed in the January 2012 issue of *Financial Planning* magazine:

1. The mind "anchors" where it shouldn't.

Anchoring describes the common human tendency to rely too heavily, or to "anchor," on one trait or piece of information when making decisions. Through the concept of anchoring, our minds attach or anchor our thoughts to a reference point, even though that reference point may have no logical relevance to the decision at hand. During normal decision making, anchoring occurs when individuals overly rely on a specific piece of information to govern their thought processes. For example, when a person decides to buy a used car, he or she may focus excessively on the odometer reading and model year of the car, especially if these criteria were learned and used in previous thought processes. This person uses the criteria as a basis for evaluating the value of the car, rather than considering how well the engine or the transmission has been maintained.

Anchoring can also be a source of frustration in the financial world when investors base decisions on irrelevant figures and statistics. For example, some investors invest in the stocks of companies that have fallen considerably in a short amount of time. In this case, the investor is anchoring on a recent "high" the stock achieved, believing that the drop in price provides an opportunity to buy the stock at a discount. However, stocks quite often also decline in value due to changes in their underlying fundamentals. For instance, suppose that XYZ stock had strong revenue in the last year causing its share price to shoot up from $25 to $80. Unfortunately, one of the company's major customers, who contributed to 50 percent of XYZ's revenue, decided not to renew its purchasing agreement with XYZ. This change of events causes a drop in XYZ's share price from $80 to $40. By anchoring to the previous high of $80 and the current price of $40, the investor erroneously believes that XYZ is undervalued. In this example, the investor has fallen prey to the dangers of anchoring.[9]

2. The mind wants to be right and avoid being wrong.

People like to be right and seek out information to prove they're right. People also like to avoid the embarrassment and any sense of personal degradation from being wrong. So, they rationalize away whatever information that suggests they're wrong. This pitfall is referred to as the confirmation bias.

3. The mind prioritizes information that's prominently available.

When purchasing a car, are you more likely to purchase based on 1,000 anonymous consumer reviews that rate it highly, or based on complaints from your neighbor, who just purchased the car and it turned out to be a lemon?

---

[9] *http://www.investopedia.com/university/behavioral_finance/behavioral4.asp#ixzz1x 544IznF*

4. The mind can see 20/20 in hindsight.

How could anyone have missed the bubble in the housing market? Wasn't it obvious? Hindsight is 20/20, and revisionist history is rampant when money is on the line, making people believe that an outcome is more obvious once it is already known. The perceived ability to spot a bubble after the fact is a great example of hindsight bias in action. Few people in 1999 or 2008 were forecasting that the bubble in financial markets would burst. Yet, looking back on the two bubbles, many people feel that, at the time, they actually "saw all of the signs" that the bubbles would burst. The human mind has a tendency to forget the many reasons why it did not seem so obvious at the time.

5. The mind loves to play "mental accounting" games.

Do you treat "found money" differently from earned income? Many people spend tax refunds or bonuses more frivolously, even though money is money. Watch out for mental accounting. For example, logically speaking, money should be interchangeable, regardless of its origin. Treating money differently because it comes from a different source violates that logical premise. Where the money came from should not be a factor in how much of it you spend, regardless of the money's source. Spending it will represent a drop in your overall wealth.

6. The mind fears losing more than it values winning.

As mentioned previously, but also published in *Financial Planning* magazine, prospect theory in behavioral finance suggests that people fear losing about twice as much as they value winning. So people are loss-averse, rather than rational, in choosing the highest expected gain or lowest expected loss.

7. The mind wants to recognize positives immediately and defer negatives until later.

Have you ever sold winning stocks too quickly and held losing stocks far too long? Investors often feel satisfaction when their investments show a profit and look to lock in those gains. Conversely, the pain of feeling regret will prompt many to hold on to a losing position in the hopes that it will break even. To avoid cutting short great investments and holding hope for poor ones, use a set criteria for purchasing or selling stocks. Incorporate new information as it comes available. And remember Warren Buffet's counsel: "The most important thing to do when you find yourself in a hole is to stop digging."

8. The mind is prone to overconfidence.

How many times have you heard someone tell you that they are 99 percent sure about something? How many times were they incorrect? Probably more than 1 percent. Overconfidence doesn't mean everyone is a narcissist—it just means we tend to be too confident in the accuracy of our own judgments. Keep in mind that a fine line separates confidence from overconfidence. Confidence implies realistically trusting in one's abilities, while overconfidence usually implies an overly optimistic assessment of one's knowledge or control over a situation.

9. The mind expects reversion to the mean even when odds are steady.

The *gambler's fallacy* is the term for the presumption that because the roulette game landed on red an amazing 11 consecutive times, the likelihood of breaking that streak—and landing on black—is more than 50/50. The fact is the likelihood of black is always 50/50, regardless of what happened on the previous roll. In investing, the parallel concept is expecting reversion to the mean. People often assume that outperforming or underperforming securities will somehow revert back to average (the mean) over time. Sometimes it happens—but sometimes not! Some investments are simply really good or really bad.

Try to separate chance from skill. In situations of chance, know that previous outcomes should have little bearing on your decisions. When viewing past performance, try to understand the drivers of those returns and whether outperformance can continue or underperformance will correct itself.

10. The mind tends to follow the herd.

"Groupthink" stems from the fact that people feel more comfortable making decisions that they see other people making. This false sense of comfort can lead to suboptimal outcomes—to the point of asset bubbles and crashes, including the most recent housing crisis.

Groupthink, which is also referred to as a *herd behavior,* was exhibited in the late 1990s as venture capitalists and private investors were frantically investing huge amounts of money in Internet-related companies, even though most of these dot-coms did not (at the time) have financially sound business models. The driving force that seemed to compel these investors to sink their money into such an uncertain venture was the reassurance they got from seeing so many others do the same thing.

With the herd mentality, we are programmed to run in the same direction as everyone else; if everyone else is doing it, it feels safer. I would agree with this reasoning if a bear was chasing us—it would be good to run as fast as we could in the same direction as everyone else, without wasting time thinking first. However, with investing, as Warren Buffet has proven over the long run, it pays to "Be greedy when others are fearful and fearful when others are greedy." In essence, it is difficult because we have to go 100 percent against our intuition.

You may have read this list and found yourself saying, "Ah yes, I have done that before." It is easy to beat yourself up after you make a mistake, especially after realizing that it was caused by a lapse in judgment or your emotions getting the better of you. It happens to the best of us. I have a saying, "The first time you make an error, it's a learning experience. The second time you make that same error it is a mistake." By understanding these psychological pitfalls and appreciating how they may have affected you in the past, you are less likely to let them affect your decisions in the future. I think you will agree that our behaviors, in fact, do affect our investment decisions. Many times we aren't purely rational when dealing with our own financial state of affairs, and we know sometimes it is simply factors of human nature, such as fear or greed, that drive us. These factors can hinder us and detract from our goals. They can actually *thwart the achievement* of our intended goals, whether they are short term or long term.

That reminds me of a story about a client who fits this scenario because her behavior did, in fact, thwart the achievement of her goals. A client hired me shortly after the tech bubble burst in 2003.

Her portfolio consisted mainly of technology stocks and she was visibly distraught. Her portfolio had shrunk from more than $100,000 to less than $10,000. She had the likes of Acatel-Lucent that crumbled from more than $80 per share when she bought it to a little over $2 after the tech bust was over. She also had purchased JDS Uniphase for close to $900 per share only to watch the price drop to the high teens.

Unfortunately, these stocks were only two of more than a dozen that took a similar downward spiral. When we discussed her options for these stocks, she insisted that she wanted to hold the stocks until they recovered. I tried to explain to her that she may never see that day during her lifetime. But she stood by her words; she couldn't bear to sell them and admit that she had made a mistake. Ten years later, she is still holding them in her brokerage account. Unfortunately, only one of her stocks recovered to the value it was when she had purchased it. The rest are still valued at a mere fraction of what they were once worth. She still refuses to sell the remaining stocks even though she knows that she would need them to grow by, in some cases, 200 percent per year for the next 10 years, on average, just to break even.

As you ponder these pitfalls and think about how some of them may have affected your decision making in the past, keep them in mind as you make financial decisions in the future. Simply being aware of these psychological pitfalls and doing our best to avoid them will provide a better opportunity for successful investing.

FADS ARE SOMETIMES HARD TO RESIST

Fads can be confused with trends, but they are different. Trends tend to persist over the long term and are generally based on fundamentals. Think about Amazon.com (online shopping) and sporting goods, such as skateboards, being trends. While Crocs and Heelys, and the Internet sensation called "planking" would be considered fads. Fads are generally marked by temporary and excessive enthusiasm that turns out to be unsustainable. The dot-com bubble is a good example of a fad where investors were more inclined to purchase a stock if its business had even the slightest exposure to the Internet. That fad ended with the dot-com bubble burst. Many people lost fortunes.

If you get caught up in the hype, you're likely to suffer with the crash that happens to nearly every fad. I am talking about the "investments of the day," similar to some of the social networking companies. No one knows how long Facebook and Twitter are likely to stay, but social media has become the focus of a crazed fascination with highly unlikely future valuations. Social media may be just another investment fad.

> **Key Point:** *Focus on your goals. Don't become distracted by the noise of information overload, or let human-nature factors get in the way of creating your masterpiece.*

SO, WHAT'S THE ANSWER?

Just as Michelangelo always listened carefully to his mentors, he also had to be aware of others trying to give him advice. According to British art critic, Andrew Graham-Dixon, Michelangelo originally did not want to paint the 12,000-square-foot ceiling because he thought it was a ruse by his enemies to get him to fail on a grand stage. He kept turning it down, saying, "I'm a sculptor, not a painter," according to Diane Apostolo-Cappadona, a Georgetown University professor who has studied his work extensively. Ultimately, as we know, he changed his mind and created a masterpiece of sublime beauty.

The point is, with so much information available to the average investor, it is sometimes difficult to know what information to rely on as objective, independent, and newsworthy versus emotion-driven opinions that point in different directions and leave you scared like a deer in the headlights. Understanding the basics of behavioral finance (and avoiding those behaviors discussed previously) will lead to good self-awareness and make it easier for you to filter out the noise.

Additionally, some information provided to us can be self-serving for the person providing the guidance. Having the awareness, like Michelangelo did, can help you differentiate those truly trying to help you and avoid those offering poor advice.

You won't find shortcuts to making important financial decisions that will affect your life, now and during your retirement. You won't get rich by listening to the experts on television because their advice is general and does not take into consideration your individual situation and goals. Plus, much of the "advice" is short-term and short-lived. It is just part of the "noise" that we elaborated on earlier.

Someone once said to me, "You don't know what you don't know." Just being aware of the behaviors as well as the caveats listed in this chapter will be helpful as you continue on your journey to learn more about planning your financial future. The late British psychiatrist, R. D. Laing wrote this interesting explanation about not knowing what we don't know, "The range of what we think and do is limited by what we fail to notice. And because we 'fail to notice that we fail to notice' there is little we can do to change until we notice how failing to notice shapes our thoughts and deeds."[10] I hope I have given you some insight into "noticing" and understanding the overloading of information by our news outlets.

---

[10] http://www.goodreads.com/author/quotes/4436873.R_D_Laing

3 | The Blank Canvas

"Every block of stone has a statue inside it and it is the task of the sculptor to discover it."

—Michelangelo

WHAT IS RETIREMENT PLANNING? IS IT JUST THE EXERCISE OF CRUNCHING numbers to make sure you have saved enough money? No, it is much more than number crunching! It is also planning what you will be doing during your retirement years . . . *life* planning.

What will you being doing in your eighties and nineties? While some may be planning their next trip abroad or learning a new language, others may believe they will be just too old for a new adventure. Granted, you may not be physically able to run a marathon or have an interest in learning how to speak Mandarin when you are 85 years old. That's understandable! But I believe that staying physically and mentally active is one of the keys to a long *and fulfilling* life.

During your working years, your career or raising a family may have provided you with a sense of accomplishment or purpose. But after your career is over and you retire, what is going to fill this void? Quite possibly, it may be a void that doesn't need to be filled. You might have other passions such as volunteer work, hobbies, or traveling that replace this need and will provide a sense of fulfillment. My point: understanding yourself and what motivates you to jump out of bed each morning is just as important as having a seven-figure investment account.

Michelangelo, who lived a long and fulfilling life of 89 years (the average life expectancy was only 35 years in this time period[11]), was fortunate. He was able to work his entire life doing something that brought him great wealth, fame, and most importantly, purpose. In the last 30 years of his life, he started his third career in architecture! Eventually, at the age of 71, he became the chief architect of St. Peter's Basilica.[12] Maybe you won't be designing a basilica for a pope when you are in your seventies or eighties, but it is okay to continue working if that is what provides you with satisfaction and an inner sense of happiness. Maybe you want to retire as soon as you can and get out of the "rat race." As you will learn in this chapter, it doesn't matter. What matters is that you are passionate about *something*.

Your retirement is a blank canvas waiting to be painted. You have many colors from which to choose, and your options are virtually unlimited. If you think about your life as a painting, you will realize that it is never static, perhaps never completely finished, and full of depth and texture. Lived well, your life (your masterpiece) is a unique and personal expression that increases in emotional value and worth, well into your retirement years.

What if an artist was going to paint your life's story on the ceiling of your home, what would it look like (besides the fact that when you go to sell it, the new homeowners may find it a bit creepy)? Did it capture all of your accomplishments? Your victories? Your agonies of defeat or loss? Imagine for a moment what *your* "masterpiece of life" would look like.

The goal of this chapter is threefold: We will help you think about the "why" of retirement, help you get to know what "type" of person you are, and help get your "juices" flowing to assist you in thinking about what you want to do in the future.

---

[11] *http://homepage.ntlworld.com/davidjstokes/1600.htm*

[12] *http://abclocal.go.com/wpvi/story?section=news/technology&id=5045089*

WHY RETIRE?

Of course, no one says you *have* to retire. You don't have to retire because society tells you it is the thing to do. If working is your passion, don't quit. The key is to retire *to* something, not *from* something. Many people continue with their jobs as long as they can because they enjoy them so much. But if you decide you're ready, you can continue to do meaningful work in other areas, if you are so inclined. You may decide you want to work part time or do consulting work. You have so many options as you near retirement in the traditional sense. We'll discuss some of those options, but what is especially important at this juncture is to come to peace with your decision and plan for the source of your future cash flow. Yes, you need a plan—you wouldn't go on a long road trip without a road map. Don't move forward into retirement without a plan. Having one will help you proceed with assurance and confidence.

> **Key Point:** *It is worth repeating: The key is to retire* to *something, not* from *something.*

WHAT DOES YOUR FUTURE LOOK LIKE?

Work can be fulfilling and rewarding. We all love to receive recognition for a job well done. So if you retire, where and how will you get the recognition that is important to you? What does your retirement "picture" look like? Do you want to consult? Start your own business? Sit on a board? Become more involved in charitable and volunteer work? Expand your network of friends? Many times, laying the foundation for these activities is a lot easier while you're still on the job and have access to vital contacts and support. So be sure to keep those things in mind.

Lifestyle and demographic expert Maddy Dychtwald, author of *Cycles: How We Will Live, Work, and Buy,* said in her book that most baby boomers look at retirement as a new chapter in their lives, to meet new people and try new things, rather than as a phase of rest and relaxation. In other words, she says, "It won't be enough to just retire—we're going to *re-wire.*" In an interview in *Futurist Magazine,* she said, "People are questioning the concept of traditional retirement because a lot of people can't afford to retire. Instead, people are leaving their first career and going on to a second. We did a study on behalf of one of our clients and we asked people what they wanted to do in the second half of life; 42% said they wanted to cycle between work and leisure-time activities. People want to continue working beyond the traditional retirement age, but not as hard or as inflexible. Many want to start their own business. More than 50% of them said they wanted to try a whole new line of work."

So, if you're considering working after retirement here are some tips for you:

1. Look for work that's fun and rewarding, whether it's working for minimum wage at the zoo or sitting on a board of directors.

2. Consider the time commitments involved. You'll want a schedule flexible enough to take advantage of short-notice opportunities. If it's a job that you're not attached to financially or emotionally, quit and get another one. Job hopping is not the sin it used to be.

3. If you want to start your own business, research the market. Consider all the boring aspects that will be involved such as taxes, accounting, and zoning. Make sure you can afford it. In other words, don't jeopardize your entire retirement to start a new business.

4. Consider phasing in your retirement so you can do the things you always wanted to do—like climbing Mount Everest—while you're still vigorous enough to enjoy it.

5. Keep up with technology. It will increase your marketability and help you to stay up-to-date with advances in home, communication, and entertainment products.

6. Network. It's still the best way to find an opportunity that suits you.

WHAT KIND OF PERSON ARE YOU?

The phase of life we refer to as "retirement" is only constrained by your imagination and the means to put your imagination in motion.

Dr. Nancy K. Schlossberg, Ed.D., a world-renowned professor of counseling psychology and author of *Retire Smart, Retire Happy* and *Revitalizing Retirement*, pointed out in the February 2011 column "Transitions Through Life" in *Psychology Today* that pre-retirement baby boomers have numerous options and that no single path fits all sizes; they can be combined and they will change over time:

> **Key Point:** *Setting aside financial resources, your options for retirement are endless and only constrained by your imagination.*

> *Boomers can continue what they were doing, try something novel, search for a new path, relax and let life emerge, stay involved but as a spectator, or retreat to the couch. Based on my interviews and focus groups, I discovered that boomers are creative as they chart new paths for themselves.*

She identified six main types of boomers and gave them titles. Perhaps you see yourself in one of these categories:

1. CONTINUERS use their existing skills and interests, but in a way modified to fit retirement. *Example:* A retired professor continues to write books and give speeches.

2. ADVENTURERS see retirement as an opportunity to start new endeavors. *Example:* A researcher for a congressional committee became a massage therapist.

3. SEARCHERS explore new options through trial and error. *Example:* One woman sat on several boards and volunteered for several organizations as she tried to figure out what to do with the rest of her life.

4. EASY GLIDERS enjoy unscheduled time, letting each day unfold. *Example:* As one retired bank teller said, "I worked all my life. It is now my time to just chill out."

5. INVOLVED SPECTATORS care deeply about the world, but engage in less active ways. *Example:* A museum curator still follows the art world, but no longer works in it.

6. RETREATERS take time out or disengage from life. For some, this is an opportunity to think quietly about the future; for others it is a retreat from life, leading to depression.

TURNING THEIR DREAMS INTO REALITY

As we share real-life stories from individuals who are living *their* dream, hopefully their stories will inspire and motivate you to find *your* dream.

Use Your Business Skills to Better Improve a Nonprofit

When successful businessman John K. Hoey was invited to lead one of the fastest-growing, large metropolitan YMCA associations in North America, he wanted to give the invitation time to sink in. Said Hoey, "I never had a master plan to transition from the corporate world to running a charitable organization like the Y. I just assumed I'd spend the rest of my career in the corporate world and continue serving on nonprofit boards, doing my part that way. I very much loved what I was doing in the business world. I had been in the for-profit education business for 11 years and had an opportunity to experience a lot of interesting and gratifying things; I helped to start businesses, ran businesses, and did lots of interesting things all over the world."

Hoey, previously an executive with Citicorp (now Citigroup) for eight years and a long-time community volunteer, also had this to say: "There was something about this opportunity that was both compelling on a business level as well as on a personal and community level."

As a preretiree, Hoey has given a lot of thought to his pre-and postretirement years. "I think I am a lucky guy because I get to come to work every day and do something I really love, something that has an important impact on the community, and I haven't had to put my business skills on the shelf to do that." This aspect of his job change is something that prevents some preretirees from making a change from a profit to a nonprofit organization: believing that their business skills might not be put to good use, either before or after they retire.

Also, before making a transition, it's important to have your retirement plan in place so you can have some financial confidence, especially if your income level will be lower. "I was very cognizant of the financial implications of the transition I was making, and I worked hard on that side of the equation before I made my final decision. Of course, I walked away from some upside potential like equity opportunities and such, but the Y is a big organization and I feel as though I am compensated fairly, that I am leading the kind of life I want to lead and that I have a solid retirement plan in place. I also have a plan in place for my kids' education."

When asked for some words of advice for those nearing retirement, he commented, "I would say to preretirees that you need to have a plan to be engaged somehow in something else after retirement. You see people who retire and they don't have a purpose anymore. They really struggle. To be successful in retirement, find some things that you love to do. It is a transition, but you can only play so much golf. Find a way to occupy your mind and your passion. That is what I would recommend."

Use Your Expertise by Helping Those Less Fortunate

We've all heard the stories about doctors, nurses, dentists, and other medical professionals who take time during their careers to do volunteer work and help underprivileged children and the elderly. Many find it rewarding to help relieve the suffering of others. I recently read an article in *Ocular Surgery News* about a retired Navy ophthalmologist and optician who traveled to Kenya on a volunteer medical mission on behalf of the World Blindness Outreach (WBO) organization.[13] The WBO is a humanitarian organization that supports eye missions to treat correctable blindness and preventable eye diseases among indigent peoples throughout the world.

Teresa Risley, a retired optician from New Orleans, who is a longtime Rotary International member and also the Avoidable Blindness Task Force chair for her Rotary district said, "We expressed an interest in partnering with vision groups going to Africa, and they paired us with Dr. Albert Alley, the co-founder and president of WBO." She

---

[13] *http://worldblindnessoutreach.org/Article_Kenya.html*

continued, "I was actually the non-medical coordinator for the team."
Dr. Dennis Pratt, a retired Navy ophthalmologist from Norfolk,
Virginia, was the only other American doctor to go on the mission.
Dr. Pratt, who started working with WBO in 1995, now goes on eye
mission trips whenever he can, which consists of performing cataract
surgeries among other things.

"I had learned of Dr. Alley's work and even covered his practice in
1994 during a mission trip," explained Dr. Pratt. "I was hooked after
my first time!" Risley was quoted as saying, "This was a life-changing
experience and since returning, I have reordered my priorities, trea-
suring simple things like never before, and want to do more eye mission trips!"

The volunteer American doctors (some retired, some not) help
train the medical team of Kenyan doctors on equipment used during
the surgeries, as well as perform and assist with the surgeries. On one
medical mission, 500 surgeries can be performed in one week, and
with the donated supplies, 500 more operations can be performed
by the Kenyan doctors. Rotary International contributed $35,000 to
subsidize the materials needed to perform 1,000 cataract surgeries in
Kenya on that particular mission. Teresa Risley and Dr. Dennis Pratt
explained that helping change lives is an awesome feeling, and in their
retirement they are feeling extremely rewarded.

Turn Your Hobby into a Business

Retirees looking to boost their bank accounts or those wanting to
give back to the community may be able to do both with a hobby
they already enjoy. We are hearing more about retirees turning their
life-long passions into retirement careers. Whether they love arts and
crafts, photography or cooking, they can find ways to turn a hobby
into retirement income and have lots of fun, too. It all starts with a
dream and a plan. Hobbies such as knitting, painting, poetry writing,
woodworking, gardening, and even traveling are good examples of
potential retirement careers. For example, if you love to travel as a
hobby you could use your travel adventures as a travel writer or book
author. I read recently about a gentleman who loved building and

repairing computers, so after retirement he set up a computer building and repair business at home. A former banker in San Diego turned his love of local history into a tour business. If you love gardening or landscaping you might become a landscape designer, or if you enjoy baking, you can start a local cookie-making business and sell online. The added bonus is that if it's a hobby, it's not like working, it's about having fun doing what you love doing.

Here is a great example of someone doing just that: In the fall of 2011, *ABC News*[14] featured Richard Druckman, a 72-year-old man and an executive at Bristol-Myers Squibb for 35 years, who retired and pursued his lifelong hobby of photography. He was actually an amateur photographer who created family calendars, but liked it so much he wanted to do it full time, and perhaps even start a small business. So, in 1984 while on a family vacation in Los Angeles, he decided he wanted to become a freelance photographer.

During the *ABC News* interview, he said that he truly believed his photography could also be more than a hobby, that he could make money doing it. So he set out to take a lot of great, professional-looking shots and tried to get them published. "While I was working, I was taking classes, I subscribed to every photo magazine," said Druckman. "I found a gentleman by the name of Bill Eppridge who was an old-time *Time Life* photographer who worked for *Sports Illustrated*. I basically called him, told him what I was doing and asked, 'Would you be willing to coach me and teach me everything you know?'"

Druckman has had surprising success for a late bloomer in a competitive field. His sports images—from Michael Phelps winning his first Olympic gold to Michael Jordan playing his last home game—have appeared in newspapers across the country and in *Sports Illustrated*. Even though Druckman retired from the corporate life, he said he was never going to retire from doing what he loves—taking pictures of great athletes.

---

[14] *http://abcnews.go.com/US/Jobs/businessman-retires-turns-photography-hobby-successful-act/story?id=14623573*

Do What You Love; Love What You Do

Paul Yarbrough, a published author of short stories and a new novel called *Mississippi Cotton*, which he says is "largely biographical," has had a successful 35-year career as a company man and a consultant in the oil business in Houston. When asked if writing is his second career, he said, "Well, I never even thought of having a traditional retirement. What, and do nothing? No one should *ever* do nothing!"

He said he began writing about 10 years ago in the evenings after work and then, at around "retirement age," he officially began collecting Social Security benefits. He explained that he still has not retired "officially," and he still does some consulting work while spending most of his time writing these days. As a matter of fact, he has already completed his second book, *The Tennessee Walls*, and is working on his third book, *A Mississippi Whisper*.

How does he feel about his financial situation now that he spends the majority of his time writing novels instead of collecting full-time consulting fees? He said that while he is comfortable financially, he is "no T. Boone Pickens," but he is really enjoying life. "Writing is my hobby but, sure, I would be happy if I can make money at it, too. That's a bonus!" Yarbrough seems to be on the road to making money selling his books. He has done book signings at Barnes & Noble bookstores and during various book tours. His book has been nominated for several national literary awards, as well. But does he miss the corporate life? Said Yarbrough, "My writing work is more fulfilling because it's always a new adventure. And I love when people read my stories and enjoy them. It's very rewarding."

Yarbrough gave some advice to preretirees who are not sure what to do after retiring, or who are insecure about exploring new avenues or having new adventures. "Find what you want to do, but don't spend a lot of money doing it. It's really not necessary. Just don't be idle." He continued, "If people retire and just sit around the house with their spouse and do nothing but watch TV all day, it could hurt their marriage. You wind up getting in each other's way. You see, I really don't feel like we were meant to retire and just do nothing." Yarbrough suggests finding your passion and following it.

TIME TO REFLECT

Retirement isn't the cessation of your life's activities and experiences as you know it. You want to continue doing the things you love, whether it means working longer because it's your passion, volunteering, turning your hobbies into businesses, or traveling to places you've always dreamed of visiting. As I mentioned earlier, the key is to retire *to* something, not *from something*. You have so many options as you near retirement, and we've shared some of those stories (or options) from people who are living their dreams beyond the traditional retirement.

Retirement creates an opportunity for you to not only spend more time on your existing hobbies and interests, but also to find *new* hobbies and adventures. As you try new things in life, you may even find you have a hidden talent.

According to an article[15] titled "Painting Is Not My Art," by William E. Wallace in *The Wall Street Journal,* Michelangelo wrote of his travails in an acerbic sonnet: "My beard to Heaven. My chest bent like a harp. The dripping brush making a rich pavement of my face. My loins have been shoved into my guts, my butt is ballast." At the bottom of the sheet, he complained, "I'm not in a good place, nor a painter." The article continues, "Michelangelo had no previous experience directing a large-scale campaign in the demanding medium of fresco, but here he employed more than a dozen painters and craftsmen to help carry out the herculean project: hauling water up 65 feet of treacherous ladders, slaking lime for plaster, grinding and mixing pigments, pricking [scratch coating] and transferring preparatory drawings, and painting miles of architecture and ornament."

Michelangelo was willing (and able) to try something new. Of course, if a pope seeks your assistance, it would be difficult to say "no." Regardless, he used his skills and knowledge for improving his world, even though he was not comfortable with painting.

What is the moral of this story? With a willingness and commitment, you can make a difference in the enjoyment of your life and possibly others. You don't need to be an artist to do it. Nor do you

---

[15] *The Wall Street Journal*, November 17, 2012.

have to be of superior intellect or have a medical degree. We have included a few tools for you in the back of the book to help you with your retirement vision, and maybe help you find a hidden talent like Michelangelo did when he started painting.

Find something you are passionate about and go for it!

As Michelangelo would say, *"A beautiful thing never gives so much pain as does failing to hear and see it."* Reflect on what you want to do in retirement, hear it, see it . . . and *live it!*

Appendices in Back of Book

4 | *David* Is More Than 500 Years Old

> *"I am laboring in that art that God has given me in order to extend my life as long as possible."*
>
> —Michelangelo

Aᴛ ᴛʜᴇ ᴛɪᴍᴇ ᴏꜰ ʜɪꜱ ᴅᴇᴀᴛʜ, Mɪᴄʜᴇʟᴀɴɢᴇʟᴏ ʜᴀᴅ ᴍᴀɴʏ ᴜɴꜰɪɴɪꜱʜᴇᴅ sculptures. According to the book, *Michelangelo: The Achievement of Fame* by Michael Hirst, he left many of these behind because he would stop working when he thought he had learned what he needed to learn. Fortunately, he was able to finish the statue of *David* in 1504, which is now more than 500 years old.

Preserving this masterpiece would take a thoughtful and well-designed plan, so in 2008, a method was proposed to insulate the statue from the vibration of tourists' footsteps at Florence's Galleria dell'Accademia, to prevent damage to the marble.[16] Like Michelangelo's *David*, our own masterpiece also requires the creation of a thoughtful and well-designed plan that will be preserved through the generations. It becomes our legacy that has the potential to last forever.

Leaving a legacy is not always about leaving money to heirs, charities, universities, hospitals, or other organizations. Of course, these are meaningful goals for those who have enough wealth to allow their money to

---

[16] "Michelangelo's *David* 'may crack'," *BBC News* (September 19, 2008), *http://news.bbc.co.uk/2/hi/europe/7626093.stm*

make a difference for humanity. But leaving a legacy is also about how we want to be remembered by our family and future generations.

WHAT IS LEGACY PLANNING?

So how do you even begin to think about planning your legacy? Well, it doesn't necessarily have to be complicated. Legacy planning is comprised of two elements: traditional estate planning (i.e., will, durable power of attorney, living will, etc.) and the not-so-common creation of an ethical will. Ethical wills trace their history back thousands of years. They have long been a part of both Christian and Jewish culture, and can also be found in other cultures, too. Simply speaking, ethical wills are a type of "love letter" you write to your family and friends, which allows you to leave "a part of yourself" with them after you are gone. An ethical will is not meant to replace your will and is not a legally binding document; it is meant to complement your will.

As you start thinking about your legacy, you need to "begin with the end in mind," which is one of the "Seven Habits" that the late Stephen R. Covey discussed in his book, *Seven Habits of Highly Effective People*. In other words, if you had the ability to write your own eulogy, what would you want it to say? According to Dr. Covey, "The desire to leave a legacy is our spiritual need to have a sense of meaning, purpose, personal congruence, and contribution." Where would you want to be in the minds and hearts of your loved ones? Where would you want to be financially? What would you want to be remembered for? What will be your legacy? To answer these questions, we will discuss the following:

- Determining what is important to you and how you want to be remembered, including your values, proud moments, accomplishments, and priceless memories.

- Tools and ideas to help you pass along these important parts of your life to future generations.

- A discussion of the traditional aspects of legacy planning—financial and philanthropy—including legal documents.

INTROSPECTION

Throughout my career, I have always found the dichotomy of inheritance views interesting. Many clients say they are not interested in leaving money to their heirs. Have you ever seen the "I am spending my kid's inheritance" bumper stickers? On the other hand, other clients say they don't want to spend any money so they could pass their wealth down to their children and grandchildren. Of course, attitudes and opinions fall all along the continuum between these two extremes.

Unfortunately, for many people, legacy planning is mainly focused on the transferring of wealth. It is uncommon, in the media as well as in conversations with financial professionals, to discuss nonfinancial topics, such as passing values on to one's heirs. I believe people are truly interested in doing so, but are not sure what the process is, what tools are available, and which professional or service provider to call on for help. The Allianz American Legacies Study,[17] which is based on interviews of 2,627 baby boomers and their parents conducted in July 2005, discovered that nonfinancial items like ethics, morals, and faith are ten times more important to both boomers and their parents than the assets being inherited. However, according to Mark Colgan, the founder of Plan Your Legacy, "Ethical wills and legacy planning are becoming ever so slightly more common, but there is still a long way to go before they are recognized by the average person."

> **Key Point:** *Although adult children are more interested in learning traditions and wisdom from their parents, more efforts are spent on wealth transfer.*

A sculptor molds and shapes clay to create a vase, glass, or piece of art. Like a sculptor, your life has been shaped and molded by your experiences. During your lifetime, you may have had the opportunity to either pass these values along to your family or reminisce about your life's experiences and lessons. However, you may not have "gotten around to it yet." In either case, spending time, through introspection, will allow you to make sure that those cherished beliefs and memories are not forgotten.

---

[17] *https://www.allianzlife.com/NewYork/PDF/LegaciesOverview.pdf*

HOW WILL YOU BE REMEMBERED?

What information do you want to make sure is passed on to future generations so your legacy can survive your life? You will want to ponder a few core ideals and considerations, including your values, accomplishments and proud moments, and priceless memories.

Your Values

When you begin reflecting on such things as your values, as well as your desire to pass them on to future generations, legacy planning becomes significant in your life. So let's talk specifically about the kinds of things that can become a part of your legacy. First, you might agree that your legacy is more than just the money—more than leaving your wealth to your heirs. It's also about your values, such as integrity, ethics, honesty, dependability, compassion, kindness, and those sorts of things. It's also about your interests and where your heart lies, for example, family and friends, patriotism, philanthropy, spirituality, religion, world hunger, animal welfare, the homeless, and so on. Your values influence your attitude and behavior and are a reflection of your principles. They speak to what you feel is of the greatest importance.

Although this list is certainly not a complete one, it should get your thoughts flowing. Think about the following questions:[18]

1. How do you define true success?
2. What core values are most important to you and why?
3. What have you done in life to stand up for your values?
4. What does spirituality or religion mean to you?
5. If there was a gathering of your friends and family, years after you passed away, what would you like to see going on and what would you like to hear them talking about?

---

[18] *www.planyourlegacy.com*

Accomplishments and Proud Moments

Now is also the time to reflect on what you have accomplished in life and your proudest moments. They include the milestones and discoveries that have shaped your thoughts and actions. Just think, wouldn't it have been interesting to know what your great-great-grandparents achieved in their lives? Hopefully, by going through this exercise, your memory will truly "live" for generations to come. Here are a few more questions you might want to think about:[19]

1. What one person do you admire the most and why?
2. Name an event that changed your life and what the impact was.
3. What are some things you have done that you are most proud of?
4. What have your life experiences taught you (e.g., about love, relationships, family, money, facing challenges, pursuing your passion, etc.)?
5. What things might you have done differently if you had a second chance? Why?

As I write this book, I am 41 years old. I have had many proud moments. Like all parents, watching my kids excel in school and sports makes me very proud. But as I think back to my proudest accomplishments and events that have changed my life, one stands out: In 2003, my wife, Lee, and I found out that her mother had cancer. We wanted to do something to show her we cared and to inspire her to be strong. My wife and her sister, Pam, decided that they were going to run a marathon, whichmeant that Pam's fiancé and I were going to be running a marathon, *too.* At that point we were both runners, but our limit was three or four miles. If you have ever trained for a marathon, you can appreciate how much discipline goes into the training. You have to build up your stamina and strength, each week building upon the last. You start at four miles and then the next week is five miles. Five turns to six, six turns to seven, and so on. Eventually,

---

[19] *www.planyourlegacy.com*

before you know it, you are back home after a 20-mile training run and the morning has turned into the afternoon. The four of us ran the Marine Corps Marathon in Washington, D.C., in October 2004. It was something that I will never forget, and I have great satisfaction in knowing I could achieve this feat. After the run, I felt like I could accomplish anything in life! Fortunately, my mother-in-law's cancer went into remission and she is healthy again. Did our running the marathon help her? I don't know, but I have to believe that she gained inspiration from watching us train and finish the marathon.

Priceless Memories

Some moments in life are so memorable they leave an enduring imprint. For everyone who is a parent, bringing a child into this world is a special moment. But as a *new* parent, when your *first child* is born, you can't appreciate the emotions that will run through your body until you have experienced it. When my first child, Abigail, came into this world, my life changed forever. After my wife's 15 hours in labor, Abigail arrived and the doctor said to me, "Daddy, tell Mommy what you have!" At that point my eyes were so welled up with tears of joy that I exclaimed, "I don't know, I can't see anything." The doctor proudly said, "It's a girl." I cried even harder.

These kinds of moments are the priceless memories you will want to share with heirs, loved ones, and those who will follow you on the family tree. Here are additional questions[20] that will help remind you of your own priceless moments:

1. What are some of your happiest moments in life?
2. What is your most memorable childhood, family, or other story?
3. How did you meet your spouse/partner?
4. How did you feel when your child was born?
5. Tell a classic "Remember when . . ." story that is trivial, but funny and unforgettable.

---

[20] *www.planyourlegacy.com*

TOOLS TO HELP YOU PASS ON THE MEMORIES

After you have spent some time thinking about how you want to be remembered and what information you want to pass on to future generations, you'll need a process and some tools to help you organize your thoughts and, possibly, pictures.

What happens to all of your "stuff" after you have passed? Some is thrown away. Some is donated. Some may be sold. A few pictures may be hung around the children's homes. Eventually, some of the pictures and mementos will be boxed up, possibly until the next generation opens those dusty boxes.

Organizing your life's proudest moments, priceless memories, and values and beliefs in an organized format can be overwhelming. Relax. It doesn't have to be, and it could be fun! Remember, we are not trying to create a shrine; it is not going to be a room full of your belongings.

Tools to help you could include simple thing such as scrapbook-type books, videotapes, CDs, or DVDs. However, my recommendation is to keep it simple. In 50 or 150 years after you have passed away and your great-great-great-grandchild wants to know about you, technology may have changed; a videotape, CD, or DVD may be a thing of the past. However, I would bet that a book will still be a book and, while they may be read in electronic format, the language or pictures that make it up will still be used as they are today. My personal favorite is a "photobook" through Snapfish, an Internet-based photography publishing company. Remember, you are not trying to create a shrine or a 300-page memoir; you want to create a nice and simple resource that will withstand the test of time and technology, and that your heirs will use to know more about you, so your memory continues. In addition to a photo book, here are a few more ideas for you to consider:

- Legacy planning guides. Numerous templates, website tools, and instructional guides are available for use in organizing and documenting your life's proudest moments. Additional resources are located in the appendix.
- Shadow box to store your most sacred mementos.

- A website. Even though we can't predict the future of the Internet, my guess is that websites will still be around 150-plus years from now, so if you are technology savvy, you can create a website that tells your story.

Your creativity is your only constraint. A variety of commercial services can assist you with these types of projects. For example, Family Star Productions specializes in videotaping and helping with printed versions of your legacy plan. Plan Your Legacy is another service that can give you guidance. Or you can keep it simple and use Snapfish to make a photobook, my personal favorite. You might want to visit the websites listed in the appendix and see whether any of their tools might help you. Talk to your financial advisor or an estate-planning attorney about this idea and ask about resources to help you. I find this type of legacy planning meaningful and rewarding for my own clients, as well as for myself.

FINANCIAL LEGACY AND PHILANTHROPY

After you have determined how much you want to leave (or not) to people who were important to you in your lifetime, another key consideration is leaving a financial legacy to continue to support the causes that were important to you. Most people think this type of bequest is something only for the superrich to consider. But, as they say in France, au contraire. You can leave gifts, large and small, regardless of your wealth. Some strategies might include naming a charitable beneficiary in your will, giving gifts outright while you are still living, or establishing a charitable trust. Two additional ways to continue your philanthropic goals after you have passed include a foundation or donor-advised fund. As you can see, you can consider many opportunities as you plan your philanthropic legacy. You should consult with your estate attorney and other advisors to assist you with these

Key Point: *Leaving a financial legacy to continue supporting the causes important to you is a key consideration.*

strategies. Just as other sections in this book could command an entire book, this section could as well. To help you think about your options, I have included a brief description of two possible vehicles to help you achieve your goals: a foundation and a donor-advised fund.

Some of the well-known philanthropists[21] who have set up foundations or have gifted to a charitable cause include Warren Buffett, who gifted $31 billion to the Bill and Melinda Gates Foundation; Joan B. Kroc who gifted $200 million to National Public Radio; T. Boone Pickens, who gifted $500 million to Oklahoma State University; and Oprah Winfrey, who has already donated $300–400 million of her $1.5 billion fortune to many charities, including her own foundations. For example, the Angel Network gives to the Leadership Academy for Girls in South Africa. Oprah also donates to the Mississippi Animal Rescue League, HIV and AIDS causes, and Free the Children, among many others.

As I mentioned already, you don't have to be superrich to set up a philanthropy plan—you just need a willingness and know-how. Let's briefly talk about a couple of the philanthropic options that are available to you.

Private Family Foundation — A private family foundation is a separate legal entity that can endure for many generations after your death. Through an attorney, you create the foundation and then transfer assets to the foundation which, in turn, makes grants to charities you want to support. You and your descendants have complete control over which charities receive grants. But unless you can contribute enough capital to generate funds for grants, the costs and complexities of a private foundation may not be worth it. *Tip: One rule of thumb is that you should be able to donate enough assets to generate at least $25,000 a year for grants, or about half-a-million dollars.*

Just think about it for a moment, if properly set up, your great-great-great-grandchildren could be making gifts to causes, in your name, that were important to *you*.

---

[21] *www.barrons.com*

Donor-Advised Fund—Another example, one that my wife and I have employed, is a donor-advised fund. Similar in some respects to a private foundation, a donor-advised fund offers an easier way for you to make a significant gift to charity over a long period of time. An example is a community foundation that holds many of these types of accounts and manages their investment and distribution as "advised" by the donor. A donor-advised fund actually refers to an account that is held within a charitable organization. The charitable organization is a separate legal entity, but your account is not—it is merely a component of the charitable organization that holds the account. Once you transfer assets to the account, the charitable organization becomes the legal owner of the assets and has ultimate control over them. You can only advise—not direct—the charitable organization on how your contributions will be distributed to other charities.

A donor-advised fund, if properly set up, can also last for generations. For my wife and me, we wanted to teach our children about philanthropy. The donor-advised fund allows us to focus on the causes we want to support. My hope is that decades after I have passed away, my children will still use, and add contributions to, our donor-advised fund to help carry on our charitable intentions. If they have found worthy causes they are passionate about during their lifetime, perhaps they will see fit to contribute to those causes as well. Then, I hope they teach their children, and the tradition carries on for generations to come.

LEGAL DOCUMENTS

This chapter would not be complete without mention of the legal documents that every adult should have. Of course we could devote an entire book to the topic of estate planning. The purpose of this chapter is not to have a thorough discussion of the legal documents but, as you have read, to dive into the nonfinancial and philanthropic aspects of legacy planning.

With that said, it would be appropriate to take a moment and discuss traditional planning concepts because they are certainly part of legacy planning. Every adult, at a minimum, should have a will, living will, and durable power of attorney. Depending on the complexity of your situation, you should consider a team of experts to provide appropriate resources and advice. Your team should certainly include an estate planning attorney and possibly other professionals such as a financial advisor and CPA.

A LEGACY GAP?

In addition to putting your own legacy in order, you may need to help your parents with theirs. If you are a baby boomer, it may be time to talk to your parents about their plans and desires, and to let them know what is important to you. Baby boomers are positioned to benefit from the largest transfer of wealth in history, with an estimated $25 trillion moving to the baby boomer generation over the next several decades, according to the Allianz *American Legacies Study*[22] conducted by Harris Interactive. Yet the study found that only a quarter of all boomers have discussed the transfer with their parents.

This legacy gap is evident in some of the findings of the Allianz study. For example:

- 17 percent of elders believe their children are counting on an inheritance, but only 4 percent of boomers are.
- 22 percent of elders believe they owe their children an inheritance, but only 3 percent of boomers feel that way.
- 39 percent of elders say it's very important to pass along their financial assets or real estate to their children, while only 10 percent of boomers see that as a priority.

Although elders and boomers may disagree with some aspects of legacy planning and inheritance, Dr. Ken Dychtwald, president of Age

---

[22] *https://www.allianzlife.com/NewYork/PDF/LegaciesOverview.pdf*

Wave, a gerontologist, and designer of the survey, had this to say, "Many people wrongly assume the most important issue among families is money and wealth transfer—it's not. This national survey [Allianz] found that for the overwhelming majority, legacy transfer has to do with deeper, more emotional issues. An inheritance focuses primarily on the money, but a true legacy also includes memories, lessons and values you teach to your children over a lifetime."

NO BETTER TIME THAN NOW

At this time, I want you to relax, put your feet up and get comfortable. I want you to set this book down and think about what is important to you; there is no better time than right now! Find "that place" that allows you to really focus.

Grab a pen and piece of paper and start thinking. Take your time; it is not a timed test. In fact, this exercise will probably take multiple sessions.

Individually, you have developed a values system based on your own experiences in, and observations of, the world. Some people believe we came into this world with no worldly possessions and that is how we will leave it—spending or giving it away to charity, not leaving it to their children. Some believe that leaving as much to their children as possible will help future generations. What you believe doesn't matter at this point of the process. What matters is that you have an opinion of what you want to achieve.

If you are married, you may want to think about it separately and then have a discussion with your spouse about what you each want. In the event of differing opinions—one spouse doesn't want to spend any money in retirement, but instead wants to leave everything to the children and live on Social Security benefits, while the other spouse wants to leave zero to the children (spend their inheritance) and live life "to the max" during retirement—a compromise will be necessary.

Beyond the financial thoughts, consider the other aspects of legacy planning as well. Think back about your life and capture those priceless memories, proud moments, and accomplishments. What beliefs, values, and wisdom do you want to ensure are transferred to future generations?

PRESERVING YOUR MEMORY

You have spent your entire life building a reputation around your values, morality, faith, family, and friends. After you leave planet Earth, how will you be remembered? Without taking the time needed to put your legacy plan into action, your memory, like a painting, will fade. But if properly planned and executed, your legacy can last forever, just like Michelangelo's famous masterpiece, *David*.

5 | Putting the Puzzle Together

> "Our goals can only be reached through a vehicle of a plan, in which we must fervently believe, and upon which we must vigorously act. There is no other route to success."

> —Pablo Picasso

PLANNING IS THE BEGINNING OF ANY GREAT WORK OF ART OR CREATION, from St. Peter's Basilica to our own life masterpiece. It begins with a basic thought that progresses to various steps in a process, culminating in the final plan and leading to the ultimate goal. Many plans and processes went into building St. Peter's Basilica.

St. Peter's Basilica, as it stands today, was begun in 1506. The first basilica, "Old St. Peter's Basilica" was begun by the Emperor Constantine between 326 and 333 C.E. By the end of the fifteenth century, the old Basilica was falling to pieces. In 1505, Pope Julius II decided to demolish the old St. Peter's and build a Basilica that would be the grandest church in the world. He held a competition and invited numerous artists and architects to draw designs. A plan was selected and the building had begun, but Pope Julius did not get his new Basilica. In fact, it was not finished for 120 years. The construction lasted through the reigns of twenty-one popes and the many plans of eight architects. That's a lot of planning!

In 1547, Michelangelo, who was already more than 70 years old, became the architect of St. Peter's. He was the main designer of the building as it stands today. He looked at all the plans that had been drawn by some of the greatest architects and engineers of the sixteenth century. He knew he could do whatever he liked, but he had respect for the other designers.[23] Unfortunately, Michelangelo died before the job was finished, but not before the construction was completed to a point where other people could finish it. He surely had a well-designed and documented plan that allowed his ideas and dream to come to fruition.

FINANCIAL PLANNING IS MORE OF AN ART THAN A SCIENCE

In life, as with a sculpture, is it really necessary to plan everything in careful detail as you begin your masterpiece, or should you let it evolve as you go along? For example, planning a sculpture can be helpful because then you will know exactly what you're going to do, but it could also inhibit your creativity. Conversely, letting a sculpture evolve as you work allows for creativity, but also leaves you vulnerable to the possibility that it will not come to life as you hoped it would. Do you want this to happen to your own masterpiece? Your life?

Of course you don't. But how can you plan for your life, your future, when it is impossible to know what your future holds? You will be faced with many variables, such as how long you will live, whether medical expenses will play a role in your financial picture, what rate of return you will earn, and how high inflation will be. But whether you are approaching a piece of marble to sculpt or your retirement goal, you really have only two choices: to create a game plan or to "wing it." Planning for retirement, while not a surefire way to ensure enough savings for your later years, is better than winging it.

There is an art to retirement planning, and of course, there is a science to it as well. The two elements work together in harmony, just like the colors that blend beautifully on your canvas. You need to use your artistic creativity, as well as special technical skills, to achieve your masterpiece. You do not achieve it haphazardly with your eyes closed.

---

[23] *http://simple.wikipedia.org/wiki/St._Peter%27s_Basilica*

PAINTING WITH YOUR EYES CLOSED

I am amazed at how many people approach retirement planning with
less thought than they do when buying a new car. In fact, according
to Thomas J. Stanley and William D. Danko, co-authors of *New York
Times* best-selling book, *The Millionaire Next Door,* "There is an inverse
relationship between the time spent purchasing luxury items such as
cars and clothes and the time spent planning one's future." This notion
is truly astonishing, and I wonder why it is true. Could it be that it
is easier to pick out a new car? Is it more fun to buy a new car? Is it
because people don't know how to plan for their future?

Among the many possible reasons, I
would surmise some people may not even
know what financial or retirement planning really means. They might believe
that true planning of any kind is no better
than just a few good guesses. Of course,
they either might not trust anyone to do
planning for them, they do not personally
know a skilled financial professional who
can help them, or they don't know how
to find one.

> **Key Point:** *Finances
> may make you un-
> comfortable. Pro-
> crastination and
> avoidance are easy to
> justify when you are
> uncomfortable. Spend
> time planning.*

Now, let's discuss the following:

- Various ways to plan
- The advantages and disadvantages of saving too much
- Spending retirement assets with confidence
- Financial planning and retirement income strategies
- Tools available to both investors and advisors

These topics will give you a nice overview of what is involved in
the process of financial planning.

Too often people become consumed with counting every penny
and end up missing out on living life. Or perhaps they feel that tomor-
row isn't guaranteed so they live life "to the fullest" without planning

for the future, ending up with nothing. Like anything in life, it's all about balance and perspective.

> **Key Point:** *Planning can help you find that fine balance between living for today and saving for your future.*

RULES OF THUMB

Using a rule of thumb to plan for what may be considered the most important goal of your life is better than not planning at all. While the following discussion may be widely known and mentioned in financial publications, it does not necessarily mean they should be considered in your situation—remember, they are just rules of thumb.

Save the Most That You Can and Then Be Frugal

Did you question the preceding statement, the one about the "advantages and disadvantages of saving too much"? Perhaps I should have said: What are the advantages and disadvantages of not being able to spend the money you've saved for retirement? That's better. You certainly want to enjoy your retirement, but some may say that the fear of running out of money can get in the way of enjoying retirement. Even if you do have enough, perhaps you won't spend it because your fear is simply too great. Many people find that when they retire they don't really enjoy their money because they are still in a saving mode, pinching all of their pennies. They are no longer obsessed with *saving* for retirement; they are obsessed with *hanging on to* every penny. Sadly, now what happens is they spend their retirement years hoarding money, scared the money will run out before they die. Of course, this concern is legitimate. While having financial discipline and saving money are crucial, it is also good to have the confidence to know you can spend on occasion to get some enjoyment from the material items and experiences it can purchase. As I mentioned earlier in the book, money can't buy happiness; however, if you plan well you can spend some of that money during your retirement, and it can help you do the things you want to do in life that will provide real pleasure.

The 10 Percent Rule: Now Becomes the 20 Percent Rule

Saving 10 percent of your income was a good traditional rule popularized in the 2004 book by George Clason, *The Richest Man in Babylon*. The rule was that if you save 10 percent and invest it with long-term returns of about 10 percent your investment portfolio will grow to the point it can support your lifestyle from its earnings in roughly 35–40 years. However, given the worldwide economy over the past decade and your time horizon if you are nearing retirement, you need to take a look at extending that 10 percent rule. You could strive to save a *minimum* of 10 percent of gross income annually, BUT I highly recommend that you target saving 20 percent, ultimately.

The benefit of saving 20 percent is that it forces you to live on 80 percent of your income, which is helpful when retirement time comes. For example, if you earn $100,000 per year and save $20,000 for retirement, you'll live on $80,000 (less taxes). By the time you retire, you are then used to living on $80,000, not $100,000.

> **Key Point:** *Living below your means while you are in accumulation mode will ultimately help you prepare for retirement.*

Rule of 25, or the 4 Percent Rule

Don't withdraw more than 4 percent of your savings per year. In 1994, William Bengen, an MIT grad and financial advisor, backtested a 4 percent withdrawal rate with a balanced portfolio of U.S. stocks and government bonds earning overall market returns, as represented by the S&P 500 index and 5-year Treasury notes, and he found that a person could safely withdraw 4 percent of his or her portfolio during any 30-year period since 1926.[24]

The general idea is that if you have a portfolio with a 50/50 asset allocation of stocks and bonds, you can withdraw 4 percent of the

---

[24] *http://www.forbes.com/sites/williampbarrett/2011/05/06/all-about-the-4-rule-for-re tirement-spending/*

portfolio each year with only a small chance of running out of money somewhere down the line. A 4 percent withdrawal rate would be $333/month for each $100,000. However, your portfolio will experience wilder swings, and this rigid method is especially sensitive to the returns in the first years of retirement. If you have a bad decade upfront, your chance of going broke rises quickly.[25]

The Million $ Retirement Rule

For many, $1 million is the magical number to have saved for retirement. But for some people, it will not be enough because $1 million is just not what it used to be. With people living longer and the continuing rise in the cost of living, $1 million no longer guarantees a five-star retirement. It also depends on the lifestyle you want to maintain and where you live or where you want to live after you retire. According to the RETIRE Project from Georgia State University, most retirees need more than 75 percent of their preretirement income to maintain their same standard of living. For example, at $90,000, the highest salary level examined, a married couple would need to have $70,200 of annual retirement income, or 78 percent of preretirement salary, to maintain the couple's standard of living during their initial years of retirement. Furthermore, these dollar amounts will need to be greater in later retirement years, commensurate with increases in the cost of living (inflation). Households earning less than this needed a higher percentage, because they generally save little for retirement and pay much less tax while working.[26] Figure 5.1 shows additional income levels for both married couples and single individuals.

---

[25] The backtesting example is hypothetical and is for illustrative purposes only. No specific investments were used in this example. Actual results will vary. Past performance does not guarantee future results.

[26] ©2011, by Trustees of Boston College, Center for Retirement Research. By Alicia H. Munnell, Francesca Golub-Sass, and Anthony Webb.

Percent of Pre-Retirement Earnings Required to Maintain Living Standards, 2008		
Pre-Retirement Earnings	Two-Earner Couples	Single Workers
$20,000	94	88
$50,000	81	80
$90,000	78	81

Figure 5.1: Maintaining Your Living Standard in Retirement
Source: Palmer, Bruce A. 2008. "2008 GSU/Aon RETIRE Project Report." Research Report Series 08-1. Atlanta, GA: J. Mack Robinson College of Business, Georgia State University. © 2011, by Trustees of Boston College, Center for Retirement Research.

Don't Rely on the Government

Some people don't save much for retirement because they expect Social Security to carry them through retirement. But when Social Security was introduced in the 1930s, it was never meant to be the primary source of income for retirees. As a matter of fact, before the United States entered World War II, life expectancy was just over 59 for men and slightly above 63 for women, which meant that when Social Security was implemented with an eligibility age of 65, the average American would not live long enough to access the benefit! It should be viewed as a "safety net," not the foundation of your retirement plan. According to the Social Security Administration, the average monthly Social Security benefit for a retired worker is approximately $1,200.[27] Think about that. This yearly income would put a single person just over the federal poverty line if they had no other source of income.

Here are some dismal statistics, but some you should know about nonetheless.[28] According to our Social Security Administration, out of every 100 Americans who started a career and worked to the age of 65:

---

[27] *www.socialsecurity.gov*

[28] *http://www.flrministry.com/news*

- 4 of the 100 people had achieved complete financial independence.

- 12 had a moderate income and maintained a lifestyle similar to, but less than, what they enjoyed during their working years.

- 25 were dead. They did not even make it to retirement.

- 58 were living primarily on Social Security and some small pension. Of those, 60 percent were at or below the poverty level.

> **Key Point:** *If you are younger than 40, my recommendation is to not factor Social Security into your planning; treat it like a windfall. With the concerns around the future of Social Security, it may not be around as we know it today.*

If these sobering facts don't inspire you to plan right now for your retirement, what will?

Net Worth Rule: Your Net Worth Should Equal Your Age Times Your Pretax Income Divided by 10

If you are 40 years old and have $100,000 in annual income, then by this rule your net worth should be $400,000 (40 × 100,000/10). That amount, $400,000, would be from all sources of earned wealth, net of all debt. It might include home equity (after paying off the mortgage), retirement accounts, businesses and investments, but excluding personal property. This rule of thumb[29] is easy to calculate as a benchmark and is useful since it varies by age. The larger the gap between what you have in net worth and the benchmark rule, the more you may need to focus on savings strategies. It also is important to consider carefully what parts of your net worth you are willing to spend in retirement. For example, should you consider your home equity and cash value life insurance as resources for retirement income?

---

[29] *http://fyi.uwex.edu/financialseries/files/2011/01/Retirement-Rules-of-Thumb-2.pdf*

FINANCIAL PLANNING: LET'S GET REAL

Now that I've given you some food for thought on the importance of planning, some sobering retirement statistics, and some rules of thumb, let's talk about some real basics of financial planning and what it all means. (Later in the chapter, we will get a bit more involved.) I am going to assume you have not yet retired, but even if you have already retired, this section will be insightful.

Retirement planning starts with a budget—a list of your income and expenses. Without this step, you will not be able to determine whether you have enough saved for retirement. I know, it is a tedious task and nobody likes to do it. Just take a deep breath, remember that your budget does not have to be perfect (close is good enough), and as with everything in life, just try your best.

You'll need a blank budget sheet to get started (provided for you in Appendix 5-A). To complete this exercise, you will need 12 months of your check registers, credit card statements, and bank statements, as well as income sources (wages, interest, dividends, pensions, Social Security, etc.). The goal is to capture as much of your known expenses and income as possible onto this document. Some expenses are likely to slip through the cracks, but if you take your time, you should be able to be fairly accurate (assuming you have good records).

Referring to Appendix 5-A in the back of the book, your current budget, you now need to extrapolate the amounts you believe you will be spending in retirement. Everyone's life is defined differently, and how you spend your money is determined by your own lifestyle. Just remember, you might spend more money in discretionary categories, such as hobbies and travel, and less in clothing since you may not be purchasing suits, business attire, or accessories when you are retired. Also, at this point in your life, you may not be as concerned with "keeping up with the Joneses." You might not need a new car every year, a bigger swimming pool, or the country club membership you haven't used in years. The purpose of the budget is not necessarily to put *you* on a budget, but to help you plan for the *future*. However, if you are the type of person who needs more discipline to save or to help regulate your spending, it will also be helpful for that as well.

When creating your budget and your financial plan, you will also be studying such issues as health insurance and Medicare. Because a detailed discussion

> **Key Point:** *Understanding your expenses and budget in retirement is vital to long-term planning.*

of health insurance and Medicare is beyond the scope of this book, suffice it to say that medical costs and insurance could be a significant expense in retirement. Taking time to research your options will be a worthwhile use of your time. I suggest using the following resources to research this part of your retirement budget:

- Medicare. You can find many of your answers at www.Medicare.gov.

- Employer-sponsored health benefits. Contact your employer to see if retiree medical insurance is offered.

- Private insurance. If you are retiring prior to age 65 and do not have an employer-sponsored plan, you may need to research the cost of a private policy. You can contact a health insurance company or agent for quotes.

- COBRA. You may be able to continue your group coverage after you have separated from service. A good resource is your human resources department, if you have one, or http://www.dol.gov/ebsa/cobra.html.

LITTLE-KNOWN SECRETS

According to "Michelangelo's Secret Message in the Sistine Chapel: A Juxtaposition of God and The Human Brain" by Douglas R. Fields,[30] at the age of 17, Michelangelo began dissecting corpses from the church graveyard. Fields suggests that Michelangelo was an anatomist, a secret

[30] http://blogs.scientificamerican.com/guest-blog/2010/05/27/michelangelos-secret-message-in-the-sistine-chapel-a-juxtaposition-of-god-and-the-human-brain

he concealed by destroying almost all of his anatomical sketches and notes. He used his knowledge of the human anatomy to create "secrets" in the frescos of the Sistine Chapel, some of them include:

- The depiction in *God Creating Adam* in the central panel on the ceiling was a perfect anatomical illustration of the human brain in cross-section.

- In another panel, *The Separation of Light from Darkness*, leading up the center of God's chest and forming his throat, the researchers have found a precise depiction of the human spinal cord and brain stem.

- The last panel he painted depicts God separating light from darkness. Researchers report that here Michelangelo hid the human brain stem, eyes, and optic nerve inside the figure of God directly above the altar.

Our Social Security program also has little known "secrets" that can potentially increase the amount of money you are able to receive from the system. While these "secrets" are not hidden like Michelangelo's anatomical depictions were, they are not easily found unless you research the strategies. Although these strategies can work for married couples, they don't necessarily work for everyone. For example, you and your spouse need to be of certain ages and have certain work histories to utilize them. They include using the Spousal Benefit, Claim and Suspend, and Claim Now and Claim More Later.

- The Spousal Benefit: This benefit allows the worker to file for benefits and the spouse to receive a benefit based upon the worker's retirement benefit. The greatest amount that the spousal benefit could be is 50 percent of the primary insurance amount (PIA), generally equal to the retirement benefit at full retirement age (FRA) of the worker. Note: If your spouse applies for benefits prior to FRA (and is already entitled to Social Security retirement benefits), your spouse will be deemed to be filing for his or her own benefit first and if qualified for a higher amount as a spouse, the spouse will receive a combination of benefits that equals that higher amount. (See Figure 5.2.)

- Claim and Suspend: This strategy works for one-income couples. After reaching full retirement age, an individual may claim his or her Social Security benefit and immediately suspend payments in order to allow his or her spouse to claim a spousal benefit. This strategy allows the spouse with suspended benefits to allow any future worker benefit to increase by 8 percent per year (called the delayed retirement credit).

   Example: Let's assume that John (66) was the income earner and Betty (62) was a homemaker. At age 66 (FRA), John files for his own Social Security and Betty files for a spousal benefit. John then immediately suspends his benefit and waits until age 70 to collect his benefit, increasing it by 8 percent per year. Betty would receive less than 50 percent of John's benefit because she is not yet at FRA. Meanwhile, John's benefit would have increased by 32 percent (8% per year).

- Claim Now, Claim More Later: This strategy works best for two-earner couples. This popular strategy suggests applying for social security at FRA, but suspending payments until age 70. This allows your spouse to submit a "restricted application" for spousal benefits if he or she has also reached FRA. In the meantime, you both will continue to earn delayed retirement credits on both of your worker benefits. As you both reach age 70, you will be able to reapply for the maximized benefit. Be aware that only one spouse can file and suspend so that the other can claim spousal benefits; it's not possible for both spouses to file and suspend.

   Example: Let's suppose you are married (Bob is 66 and Sally is 62). Sally chooses early retirement benefits on her own earnings and Bob chooses the spousal benefit on *her* account. He delays claiming *his* own benefit until later, say 70. Bob would receive 50 percent of Sally's benefit that she would have received as her own retirement benefit if she had waited until she was 66 (FRA).

Let's say that Sally would have received $1,600 at FRA but she only receives $1,200 since she is taking it early. Bob would receive $800 (half of her full benefit). Then, when Bob turns 70 he switches from the spousal benefit to his own benefit, including the delayed retirement credit he received for waiting.

Before implementing any of these strategies, you should contact the Social Security Administration, your financial advisor, or your CPA to review your situation.

Beyond the "secrets" of Social Security, you will face many other variables when deciding how to collect your benefits. The rules applying to the claiming of Social Security benefits can be complicated and may change in the future. Furthermore, you will need to consider many factors when deciding on when *and how* to apply for Social Security benefits. Many of these variables may be hard to quantify, such as how long you plan on living. Using your knowledge of your health (and family history), whether you plan to continue working in your retirement years, and your ability to delay receipt of this retirement income will help in the decision-making process. For example, if you are in excellent health and your parents lived into their nineties and you don't need the cash flow due to pensions, then you may be better off deferring receipt of your Social Security benefits. See Figure 5.2 for a summary of the current rules for the age you need to be in order to collect your "full" Social Security benefits.

If you were born between 1943 and 1954, your full retirement age (FRA) is 66. If you start receiving retirement benefits earlier, they will be reduced. As the chart shows, if you take them as soon as you are allowed (at age 62), they will be reduced by 25 percent. Of course, you will be receiving them four years earlier than if you waited until 66, but at some point you will hit the "crossover" when waiting would have been more beneficial. Many people live by the idiom, "a bird in hand is worth two in the bush." This notion may be shortsighted, though. If you live past the "crossover," you would have been better off (i.e., in the long run you would have collected more money from Social Security) by waiting to collect your benefits. Attempting to give

Year of Birth	Full Retirement Age (FRA)	Payment Reduction at Age 62
1937 or earlier	65	80.0%
1938	65+2 months	79.2
1939	65+4 months	78.3
1940	65+6 months	77.5
1941	65+8 months	76.7
1942	65+10 months	75.8
1943–1954	66	75.0
1955	66+2 months	74.2
1956	66+4 months	73.3
1957	66+6 months	72.5
1958	66+8 months	71.7
1959	66+10 months	70.8
1960 and later	67	70.0

Note: People who were born on January 1 of any year should refer to the previous year.

Figure 5.2: When You Can Collect "Full" Social Security
Source: AICPA Guide to Social Security Planning,
http://www.ssa.gov/pubs/10035.html#a0=1.

specific advice to you now would be a futile process; too many variables weigh into your decision.

You will definitely encounter an "art" component to selecting your strategy. For the "science" aspect of it, several benefit calculators are available on the Social Security website (www.ssa.gov) to help you estimate your future retirement benefits. You may also call the Social Security Administration at (800) 772-1213 if you have questions.

I believe Social Security is an important consideration and requires careful decision making, so working with a financial planner to guide you is advisable. The "art" of Social Security planning includes trying to determine how long you are going to live by considering your genes (parent's health issues, if any) and your own health.

THE (MOSTLY) SCIENCE (AND LITTLE BIT OF ART) OF WITHDRAWALS

Withdrawal issues are sometimes more complicated than accumulation issues. For example, your tax rate, potential early withdrawal consequences, and required distribution rules need to be looked at closely. Your CPA and/or tax advisor should be consulted in this decision-making process.

But we are putting the cart before the horse. Before deciding on which investment account (such as an IRA or taxable account) to use for retirement income, we need to know *how much* you need. Here is where the budget you created comes into play. Let's look at an example:

Suppose you will have income from Social Security of $3,500/month and a pension income of $500/month. Therefore, your total income will be $4,000/month or $48,000/year. You reviewed your check registers, credit card receipts, taxes owed (when you filed your return), and bank statements to determine that you are currently spending, on average, $7,000/month or $84,000/year. Even though some of your expenses will decrease as soon as you retire, you also have determined that your travel budget will increase by an identical sum. Therefore, you will need $3,000/month ($36,000/year) from your portfolio. Financial planning will then allow you to determine if that amount is feasible, based on prudent assumptions.

After you determine the amount of withdrawals needed to maintain your lifestyle, you need to prioritize *where* you will derive your income. As a general rule, you would typically start with the accounts that are currently taxable, also known as "nonqualified." The reason is that you are already paying taxes on the dividends and interest. Plus, the gains from sales, if the assets were held longer than 12 months, are taxed at long-term capital gains rate—typically less than ordinary income tax rates. The idea is to let the assets that will be taxed at the higher rate accumulate for the longest time. In essence, only part of a traditional IRA's principal belongs to you. The IRS "owns" the remaining portion, so the goal is to minimize its share.[31] This strategy assumes that your effective tax bracket is higher than the capital gains tax rate.

---

[31] *http://www.cbsnews.com/8301-505123_162-37841513/strategies-for-withdrawing-assets-in-retirement*

Sometimes, however, it does make sense to take money from traditional IRAs prior to nonqualified accounts. For example, consider taking withdrawals from your IRA first if your tax bracket is lower than it is anticipated to be in future years. Your tax bracket may increase as a result of an increase in your income, a drop in your itemized deductions (i.e., medical expenses, charitable giving, mortgage interest), or changes in the tax laws.

It is worth saying again: You should consider consulting with a tax advisor, and possibly your financial advisor (if you are working with one), for additional resources and guidance.

PREPARE TO MEET YOUR FINANCIAL PLANNER

So, you may have decided that working with a financial planning professional can help you with your current and future life plans—helping you choose your "colors" and create your masterpiece. This step is a big one. Remember, you are the focus of the financial planning process. As such, the results you get from working with a financial planner are as much your responsibility as they are those of the planner. Whether you want your financial planner to implement all of the recommendations you have both agreed on, or you prefer having a financial "coach" to oversee your own implementation, you still need to be up to speed on what we call the "best practices" of financial planning.

Here is a Top 10 list of the best financial planning practices for you to consider as you embark on either hiring a financial advisor for the first time or confirming that your current relationship is adequate:

Top 10 Best Practices When Approaching Financial Planning[32]

1. Set measurable goals.
2. Understand the effect your financial decisions have on other financial issues.
3. Reevaluate your financial plan periodically.

---

[32] http://www.retireonyourterms.org/?p=28

4. Start now—don't assume that financial planning is only for when you get older.

5. Start with what you've got—don't assume financial planning is only for the wealthy.

6. Take charge—you are in control of the financial planning engagement.

7. Look at the big picture—financial planning is more than just retirement planning or tax planning.

8. Don't confuse financial planning with investing.

9. Don't expect unrealistic returns on investments.

10. Don't wait until a money crisis to begin financial planning.

Set specific targets of what you want to achieve and when you want to achieve results. For example, instead of saying you want to be "comfortable" when you retire, you need to quantify what "comfortable" means so that you'll know when you've reached your goals. As you know, each financial decision you make can affect other areas of your life. For example, an investment decision may have tax consequences that are harmful to your estate plan. Or a decision about your child's education may affect when and how you meet your retirement goals. Remember, most of your financial decisions are interrelated.

Financial planning is a dynamic process; it's constantly changing to react to your changing life. Your financial goals may change over time due to changes in your lifestyle or circumstances, such as receiving an inheritance, marriage, birth, house purchase, or change of job status. Revisit and revise your financial plan with your financial planner as time goes by to reflect these changes so you can stay on track with your long-term goals. Financial planning cannot change your situation overnight; it is a lifelong process. Because it is a process, your relationship with your advisor will likely be an ongoing and evolving one. Accessibility to your advisor and his or her *accessibility to you* will be vital. If the lines of communication are not open, the relationship will not reach its full potential.

Remember, some events and circum- | **Key Point:** *Financial*
stances will be beyond your control (stock *planning needs to be* market ups and downs, inflation, interest *flexible.* rates, etc.), but don't let them derail your planning. By being proactive, you will be aware of the environment and be able to adapt your plans.

Key Point: *Financial planning needs to be flexible.*

THE SIX STEPS YOU AND YOUR PLANNER WILL FOLLOW

Before you begin working with a financial advisor, I suggest that you understand the six integral steps in the professional financial planning process as followed by experienced financial and retirement planners. Financial planning is defined by the Financial Planning Association (FPA), the largest professional financial planning membership organization, as "The long-term process of wisely managing your finances so you can achieve your goals and dreams, while at the same time negotiating the financial barriers that inevitably arise in every stage of life. Remember, financial planning is a process, not a product." The six steps of the financial planning process are crucial in implementing a successful plan. Each step is integral in the process and recommended by the Certified Financial Planner Board of Standards, and I'll define them in my own words:

1. **Establish and define the client-planner relationship.**
   Your financial planner should explain, and put in writing, the services you will receive. Then, your responsibilities and your planner's responsibilities should be defined. You will have a discussion about fees and how your planner will be paid. You will also want to know whether your planner will be paid by any outside firm for products that might be recommended. You both should also agree on how long the professional relationship will last and on how decisions will be made.

2. **Gather your financial data and understand your goals.**
   Your financial planner should ask for information about your financial situation, then mutually define your personal and financial goals, understand your time frame for results, and discuss your risk

tolerance. An experienced financial planner should gather all the necessary documents from you before offering any advice.

3. **Analyze and evaluate your financial status.**

In this step, your financial planner will analyze your information to assess your current financial situation and determine what must be done to meet your goals. Depending on what services you have asked for, this evaluation could include analyzing your assets, liabilities and cash flow, current insurance coverage, investments, or tax strategies.

4. **Develop and present financial planning recommendations and/or alternatives.**

At this point, your financial planner will offer recommendations that address your goals, based on the information you provided. He or she will go over the recommendations with you to help you understand them so you can make informed decisions. Your planner will also listen to your concerns and revise his or her recommendations when appropriate.

5. **Implement the financial planning recommendations.**

You and your planner should agree on how the recommendations will be implemented. You can decide whether you want your planner to implement the recommendations or serve as your "coach," coordinating the entire process with you and other professionals on your team, such as attorneys, CPAs, insurance agents, or stockbrokers.

6. **Monitor the financial planning recommendations.**

You need to decide with your planner who will monitor your progress toward your goals. If the planner is in charge of the process, he or she should report to you periodically to review your situation and adjust the recommendations, if needed, as you experience life transitions such as job changes, marriage, births, and retirement. Your planner understands that these kinds of transitions may affect the achievement of your goals. These shifts in your life may require asset allocation adjustments in your investment portfolios, reevaluating your risk tolerance profile, and engaging in more in-depth discussions about wealth, retirement, and estate planning.

Remember, this process requires open and honest communication, possibly with a new financial advisor you have been working with for only a couple months. This dialogue is the key to your success. Your financial advisor should be able to explain your financial plan in a way that you understand. Your financial plan is not a novel that, once read, sits on a shelf in your library; it is a working document that will be used to make sure you are on track to reach your goals. I believe all of this information gives you a concise overview of the planning process and what is expected of you (and of your planner) throughout the relationship.

FINANCIAL PLANNING SOFTWARE

I mentioned earlier in the book that I began working in the financial services industry in 1994. At that time, I was affiliated with IDS Financial Services, an American Express company that later became known as American Express Financial Advisors (its current name is Ameriprise). The company, known for its emphasis on financial planning, was a pioneer in the financial planning industry. Even with that being the case, the financial planning we did, while state-of-the-art at that time, was, in retrospect, quite simple. For a retirement analysis, we used simple static return assumptions such as "an assumed rate of return of 7 percent per year." We now have more sophisticated software that allows for testing assumptions based on actual historical returns and Monte Carlo simulation.[33]

---

[33] This problem-solving technique is used to approximate the probability of certain outcomes by running multiple trial runs, called simulations, using random variables. IMPORTANT: The projections or other information generated by Monte Carlo simulations regarding the likelihood of various investment outcomes are hypothetical in nature, do not reflect actual investment results, and are not guarantees of future results. Actual results will vary.

Technology has evolved and will continue to improve. With access to the Internet, you have many different "calculators" to assist you with your planning needs. Many of them are simple to use—with limited inputs, such as rate-of-return assumption, current retirement assets, and age of retirement—but they may not be able handle more complex and realistic life changes. For example, many retirees downsize their home (say, five years into retirement) and then use the excess home equity for retirement income. Another example may be working part time in retirement. Still another example may be an expected inheritance or windfall at some point in the future (e.g., you are 55, your parents are 90 years old, you are an only child and they have an estate of $1 million) that online calculators may not have the flexibility to include.

As the saying goes, "you get what you pay for." Even though online calculators are fun to use, will certainly give you some idea of what you may or may not be facing in retirement, and will at least get you thinking seriously about the income you need for the future, they may not have the flexibility that more complex situations require.

For many retirees, custom advice about when to take pensions, Social Security, and how much to withdraw from which types of accounts can make a big difference in the amount of after-tax retirement income that will be available to them.

Working with a financial advisor who specializes in financial planning can likely provide a more detailed analysis that can be adapted to your specific situation. A financial advisor is likely to have more sophisticated software and other tools to analyze your financial goals.

The decision of whether you use the assistance of a financial advisor to create your plan, or use online or off-the-shelf software, will be based on your preferences, comfort level with the calculator(s), and of course, the cost associated with hiring a professional to assist you. But the more important part of the process, the interpretation of the output from whichever method used, is the *art* of planning. For instance, software that determines you need to save $100 more each month for your retirement may not be able to provide you guidance, based on your unique circumstances, as to which investment or type of account (e.g., Roth vs. traditional IRA, 401(k), nonqualified account, etc.) that is most appropriate.

Ultimately, you realize that financial planning is a core component of helping you achieve your goals and enjoy a comfortable retirement. If you are not on track to achieve your goals based on your current retirement plan, you have five choices:

1. Save more, spend less now.

2. Delay your retirement date goal.

3. Budget to spend less in retirement.

4. Try to be more aggressive with your investment returns.

5. A combination of all these approaches.

If you are already on track to reach your goals, based on the planning—congratulations!

ONLY YOU CAN CONTROL YOUR DESTINY

Don't expect the U.S. government or the company you work for to take care of you. Read, listen, and learn about personal finance, investments, and retirement planning strategies. Ask for advice or help from a financial professional. In the end, your financial well-being is your personal responsibility. Control what is within your control. As I mentioned in the beginning of the chapter, no one knows what the future may hold, but we cannot leave it to chance. Developing a plan and revisiting it or adjusting your goals from time to time will be necessary.

Just as the building of St. Peter's Basilica had at least eight plans developed throughout the reign of twenty-one popes, you may go through three or four of your own. Don't be discouraged; Michelangelo passionately spent his entire life creating his masterpieces. Now it's time for you to create yours.

PART TWO

The Art of Investing

In Part I, Creating Your Masterpiece, we explored some key considerations of retirement planning and set the foundation for a discussion of investing. Hopefully you are leaving Part I with a better understanding and perspective of how you value money and define happiness. Additionally, we have explored the outside factors and behavioral characteristics that can impede your ability to be objective with regard to the economy and your own finances.

Your life is a masterpiece waiting to be painted. It can be anything you want it to be—you can sit back and relax, you can find a new hobby, travel, explore another career, or volunteer. The choices are endless. I hope the stories in Chapter 3 inspired you and opened your eyes to this exploration opportunity. We discussed ways to make sure your legacy lives on so that future generations know who you were and what you believed in. Last, we pulled it together to help you understand what financial planning is and what it is not.

Now, we will move on to Part 2 of the book, *The Art of Investing*, which will explain how to put everything we've discussed up to this point to work for you. We'll talk about the nitty-gritty of investment plans, especially those relative to your retirement success. Covered are investment strategies, products, philosophies, and processes, as well as the types of financial advisors and their various capabilities and areas of expertise. But we will not get bogged down in industry jargon and will attempt to inform and educate you in a way that will make the second part of the book just as appealing and helpful as we hope the first part was.

6 | Beauty [Risk] Is in the Eye of the Beholder

"A beautiful thing never gives so much pain as does failing to hear and see it."

—Michelangelo

T HE LITERAL MEANING OF OUR TITLE "BEAUTY IS IN THE EYE OF THE Beholder" is *the perception of beauty is subjective.* In the art world it means that everyone sees art differently. Most of us may agree that the ceiling of the Sistine Chapel is a work of exquisite beauty, but some may look at certain paintings in their local art museum and not appreciate them in quite the same way as would the person standing next to them. In fact, they might not even "understand" the paintings. Just as art is subjectively evaluated, investment risk is also subject to a similar idiosyncratic interpretation and needs to be understood.

Risk is a nebulous concept; it can mean many things to different people. It is inherently subjective—human beings evaluate risk to help them understand and cope with the dangers and uncertainties of life. We have all experienced different ways of reacting to risk, depending on what it is we have at risk, or what we have lost.

Risk may mean to you the likelihood that your investment may either lose money or not grow the way you expect. When deciding which investments are right for you, the trick is to strike the right balance between the amount of risk you're comfortable with and the return you would like to receive.

Risk has a cognitive and an emotional aspect as well. We'll talk more about the behavioral aspects in the next few pages.

The past twenty years have been a roller-coaster ride for investors. In the 1980s and 1990s, many financial advisors and investors alike discounted the importance of discussing risk. It was easy back then to shelve the topic of risk because this period produced a spectacular bull market, and almost everyone was focused on the investment rewards instead of the investment risks. Of course, risk was considered and risk tolerance was discussed briefly, but its significance was undervalued. In bull markets, the conversations would typically begin with "How much return can I earn?" and "How long will it take to realize profits?" Rarely were the questions, "How much risk will I be taking?" or "How much money might I lose?" Many put return first while risk was a secondary thought. See Figure 6.1. (Efficient frontier (EF) is discussed further in Chapter 8.)

The investment climate has changed dramatically over the past decade and the discussion of risk has been brought back into focus due to the volatility in the market. In this chapter, we will define and determine how to calculate your risk tolerance—the most important, and first, step in investing.

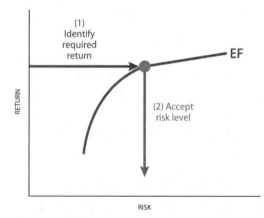

Figure 6.1: Order of Importance: Return Then Risk
Source: NGAM Distribution, L.P., Durable Portfolio Construction^SM Presentation, September 24, 2012

You see, my belief is that risk should be the primary discussion and potential return should be determined only after the risk is determined. See Figure 6.2.

In this chapter, we answer questions that must be resolved prior to investing for your retirement:

- What is risk?
- How much risk are you willing to take?
- How much risk should you take?

Hopefully, after you have finished reading this chapter, you will have a better perspective of your risk tolerance. Also, if you have a partner or spouse, you will appreciate that person's risk tolerance as well.

DEFINING RISK: IT IS ALL ABOUT THE EMOTIONS (NOT THE TERMINOLOGY)

Risk comes in many different shapes. For example, here are seven: systematic risk, unsystematic risk, interest rate risk, inflation risk,

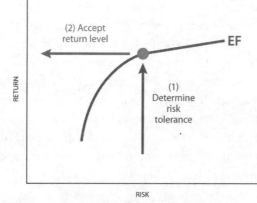

Figure 6.2: Order of Importance: Risk Then Return
Source: NGAM Distribution, L.P., Durable Portfolio Construction^{SM} Presentation, September 24, 2012

currency risk, liquidity risk, and sociopolitical risk. They are all important terms to understand as we delve deeper into discussions about investments in the book. I encourage you to take a few minutes to review the various definitions of risk on the Financial Industry Regulatory Association's (FINRA) website at www.FINRA.org. FINRA is the largest independent regulator for all securities firms doing business in the United States, and you will find the textbook definitions as well as other helpful information on risk.

Although it is important to understand the terminology, this chapter will focus specifically on developing a *sustainable* portfolio—one that will allow you to manage the *emotions* of investing so you are able to live comfortably and have financial poise, even when your portfolio is subjected to the whims of the markets. I believe that managing the emotions of investing is crucial.

> **Key Point:** *Knowledge of definitions is important but managing emotions is more important.*

Investing requires a certain level of emotional competence. You have to be even-keeled. Being "even-keeled," as it relates to investing, means that in good markets, you don't get too excited and happy, and when the market is going down, you don't become fearful.

Have you ever played poker? Controlling your emotions is a large part of the game of poker. Whether you have a royal flush or a single high card, your demeanor needs to be somewhat stoic. This behavior is required for you to periodically bluff your way to winning the pot. The skills and traits needed to be a winning poker player are much like the skills and traits needed to be a successful investor. Both are part science, part art. If you put your money in play in either arena without knowing what you're doing, you're likely to end up losing money. However, if you have a good knowledge base behind you and keep your emotions in check, you may have a better opportunity to see your profits grow. Here are few things to think about:

1. It doesn't matter if you got lucky and won a poker hand, even after completely misreading your opponent, or took an investment risk

that ended up paying off for you. Don't focus on short-term wins and losses; focus on making the best possible decisions for stable, long-term success.

2. Managing risk is a key element to being a successful poker player, as well as a key element to being a successful investor. Sometimes in poker, you may have a hand that gives you enough confidence to go "all in" or bet everything you have. It would be synonymous to having all of your retirement nest egg in one stock. A poker game has two potential outcomes: You either go home "broke" or you win the pot and continue playing. However, you have no room for error when you are investing for your retirement; going home early and broke does not work in this arena. In my entire career, I have never seen an investment (without the benefit of hindsight) that warrants an "all-in" mentality. If, in poker, you feel like you have a good hand but not enough to bet the farm, you could raise your opponent and hopefully increase the potential winnings. This approach would be similar to buying more of an investment after it falls in value (buy low). Bottom line: You may have conviction in an investment, but don't invest too much in just one investment [hand] because it is not a game, it is your retirement.

3. Know when to fold 'em. In poker, most players know that sometimes a hand that starts out with a great deal of promise just isn't worth much once the action starts to play out in front of them. In Texas hold 'em, two aces may be the best hand to start with, but knowing when they're beat and throwing them away can be the difference between winning and losing. The same is true with investing. You may start out with a great investment that has a lot of promise, but over time the fundamentals may change and the investment may not be profitable. Discerning investors have an exit strategy.

According to experts, the psychological issues that drive investing and gambling decisions aren't merely similar, "they are identical," said Andrew Lo, director of the Massachusetts Institute of Technology Laboratory for Financial Engineering and one of the leaders in

the field of behavioral finance. It's easy to find investment professionals and professional poker players who agree. Says poker pro Daniel
Negreanu, who holds four World Series of Poker bracelets and two
World Poker Tour Championship titles, "Having emotional stability
and emotional control is key to both investing and poker." Is it possible
to gain that emotional control at a poker table *and* in the world of investing? Aaron Brown thinks so. He is a onetime finance professor and
former portfolio manager for Prudential Securities (now UBS) who
is a risk manager for hedge funds. He's also the author of *The Poker
Face of Wall Street*. Said Brown in an interview, "People tell me playing
poker is risky. Investing for a financial lifetime can be risky. I'd much
rather make these mistakes at the table."[34]

I'd like to stress here that investing is not gambling. *Speculating*
is gambling. But the emotional aspects of risk taking (whether in
gambling, speculating, or investing without ample knowledge or with
uncontrolled emotions) can be enormous.

Therefore, taking a long look at and understanding the various issues surrounding
risk and risk tolerance and how human
behavior fits into the equation are essential.

> **Key Point:** Controlling
> *your emotions is vital
> when investing.*

THE CRISIS AND PERSPECTIVE

It may be difficult to remember your state of mind during the darkest
days of the financial crisis of 2008, especially after such a phenomenal
bull market we've experienced since the bottom of the market back
in March 2009. However, it's important not to let a bull market cloud
your judgment or let you forget the crisis. Try to reflect back on how
you behaved (and why) during *both* up and down markets. In those trying times, even some of the most aggressive investors had a tough time
staying even-keeled. Economists said it was the worst financial crisis
since the Great Depression of the 1930s. (The Dow Jones Industrial

---

[34] *http://www.kiplinger.com/features/archives/how-poker-can-make-you-a-better-investor.html*

Average lost 89% of its value before finally bottoming out in July 1932.)

During the financial or "credit" crisis of 2008, we witnessed the collapse of large financial institutions, the bailout of banks by national governments, and downturns in stock markets around the world. In

> **Key Point:** *It is human nature to easily forget the crisis times once we are experiencing a bull market.*

many areas, the housing market also suffered, resulting in evictions, foreclosures, and prolonged unemployment. The crisis played a significant role in the failure of key businesses and declines in consumer wealth estimated in trillions of U.S. dollars. Total home equity in the United States, which was valued at $13 trillion at its peak in 2006, had dropped to $8.8 trillion by mid-2008 and was still falling in late 2008. Total retirement assets dropped by 22 percent, from $10.3 trillion in 2006 to $8 trillion in mid-2008. During the same period, savings and investment assets (apart from retirement savings) lost $1.2 trillion, and pension assets lost $1.3 trillion. Together, these losses total a staggering $8.3 trillion.[35] Investors pulled a record $72 billion from stock funds overall in October 2008 alone, according to the Investment Company Institute, a mutual-fund trade group. Even Warren Buffett's Berkshire Hathaway Inc. reported a 62 percent drop in its 2008 net income due to investment and derivative losses of nearly $7.5 billion.[36] Needless to say, even Mr. Buffett was not immune; it was his worst year in 44 years of leading the firm.

In those kinds of volatile environments, your risk tolerance, or how *you* define risk, really matters. Textbooks cannot teach you risk; they can teach you terminology and definitions (which I mentioned before, i.e., FINRA), both of which are important to know. Similarly, risk questionnaires cannot prepare you for the emotions you may experience when your portfolio decreases in value. (We'll discuss those questionnaires in the next section—the first "puzzle piece.") The reality is that you need to be able to *experience* what the potential gain or

---

[35] *http://www.simeonnolta.com/the-great-recession/effects.html*

[36] *http://www.cbsnews.com/2100-500395_162-4835570.html*

loss *might* be. In this way, you will gain perspective and can move ahead and make intelligent investing decisions.

RISK TOLERANCE: FOUR PUZZLE PIECES AND PERSPECTIVE

So, let's begin with these two questions:

1. How much risk should you take with your investment portfolio?
2. How do you determine the amount of risk to take with your investment portfolio?

Well, I wish I could offer you an easy, cookie-cutter-type answer, but there isn't one. These types of questions make me wish I was a doctor living in a world where science determines the answer. But here, we are talking about science plus *art*. A variety of ways can be used to measure risk, such as standard deviation (the "science"). Then you run into the harder part of risk management, where things like behavior, perspective through past experience, goals, and perhaps even your time horizon, among other things (the "art"), come into play. You will find no black-and-white answers, because we live in a world of grey.

In my opinion, in order to determine your risk tolerance you need to use a combination of risk questionnaires and what-if scenarios along with a dose of perspective. Think of it as a "risk puzzle" with four pieces that need to fit together perfectly to see the total picture. They include:

1. The Questionnaire
2. The Pain Threshold
3. The Upside vs. the Downside
4. Probability of Loss

Let's take a closer look at each of these pieces.

The First Puzzle Piece—The Questionnaire

Hundreds of different risk questionnaires are currently floating around on the Internet. The real challenge is trying to determine which one(s) to use. Just like any research, questionnaire, or information on the Internet, you don't necessarily know the *quality* of the material unless you research the *source* of the material. You can do that by learning which firms in the financial services industry are credible. For example, most large mutual fund and financial services companies have sample risk questionnaires for you to use. While there are many different questionnaires available for you to use, I believe the best ones have a few commonalities:

1. They take some time to complete. They should be at least 10 questions in length; many of the best ones I have seen have 20–25 questions.

2. The questions need to make sense and avoid vagueness. For example, if the question includes a phrase something like "... you want to avoid major fluctuations," it is difficult to discern, even for an experienced investor, how to measure this loss. A better phrasing would read, "... you want to avoid '25% or more loss' in your portfolio."

3. They don't rely on rules of thumb. For example, if the questions focus solely on your age and suggest that because you are 25 years old, you should be aggressive, then it does not take into account that you may be an inexperienced investor and conservative by nature (even though you may have 40 years to go until retirement).

I have included a questionnaire offered by my firm as a sample. (See Appendix 6-A.)

In addition to researching the *quality* of the risk tolerance questionnaire and scoring measurement, it is crucial that you understand the questions and answer them objectively—and honestly. It's important for you to be candid about what makes you comfortable, as well as what makes you uneasy. When it comes to investing, understanding yourself and your risk tolerance will determine whether you'll end up sticking to your investment plan. If you don't understand a question, you should consult your financial advisor or the company that produced the document to make sure you fully understand the questions.

So now you are ready to complete the questionnaire. Hopefully, it will be a worthwhile exercise that helps you gain insight about to your risk tolerance. Remember that everyone is different, and your unique financial situation and personal preferences both affect the level of risk you are willing to take and which of the categories you fit into (see Figure 6.3). Generally speaking, there is no right or wrong answer; what's important is to examine your own situation to see what's right for you. You may even be surprised by what you will learn, and it might even cause you to make changes in your financial life, to set you on a better path to achieving your goals.

You will find that most of these questionnaires will categorize you into one of a handful of risk "types":

- **Conservative (C)** risk tolerance indicates that you are not willing to tolerate noticeable downside market fluctuations, even if that means the account does not generate significant income or returns and may not keep pace with inflation.

- **Moderately Conservative (MC)** risk tolerance indicates that you can tolerate a little more risk than a conservative investor but are still slightly averse to short-term downside fluctuations.

- **Moderate (M)** risk tolerance indicates that you want good returns and are willing to take some risk to get them.

- **Moderately Aggressive (MA)** risk tolerance indicates that you are mostly comfortable carrying a fairly high amount of risk, but don't want to lose too much in a short period of time.

- **Aggressive (A)** risk tolerance indicates that you are comfortable carrying a high amount of risk.

So, in your mind and with the understanding that more risk equals higher return potential, you should have a picture that looks like Figure 6.3:

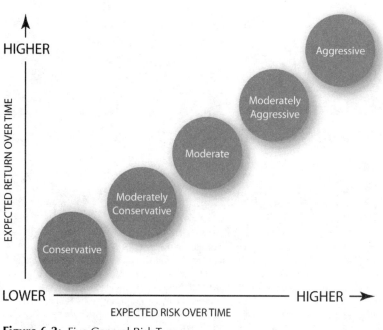

Figure 6.3: Five General Risk Types
Source: Commonwealth Financial Network; Williams Asset Management

The remaining puzzle pieces will help you confirm your questionnaire score and increase your confidence when investing.

The Second Puzzle Piece—The Pain Threshold

So now you have a completed the risk tolerance questionnaire and, based on your responses, have categorized your investment risk tolerance, along with the textbook definitions that go with each. As we have discussed, textbook definitions are a good start, but they may not completely prepare you for the "real world." The next step of this risk puzzle is to test your tolerance to make sure it was assessed accurately. Puzzle piece two, a "backtest" allows us to use hindsight to determine your reaction to market gyrations. Start by asking yourself, *"How would I react if I incurred a loss of x dollars or x percent?"* We will use inflection points of the S&P 500 for this example, but any broad-based stock market index would suffice.

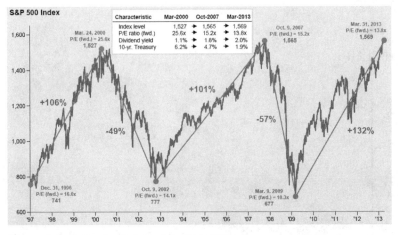

Figure 6.4: Inflection Points of the S&P 500 Index
Source: Standard & Poor's, First Call, Compustat, FactSet, J.P. Morgan Asset Management. Dividend Yield is calculated as the annualized dividend rate divided by price, as provided by Compustat. Forward Price to Earnings Ratio is a bottom-up calculation based on the most recent S&P 500 Index price, divided by consensus estimates for earnings in the next 12 months (NTM), and is provided by FactSet Market Aggregates. Returns are cumulative and based on S&P 500 Index price movement only, and do not include the reinvestment of dividends. All indices are unmanaged and investors cannot actually invest directly into an index. Unlike investments, indices do not incur management fees, charges, or expenses. Past performance does not guarantee future results. Data as of 3/31/13.

When running this what-if scenario, my suggestion is to think about or have dialogue with your financial advisor about the inflection points (positive and negative) of the S&P 500 (Figure 6.4) or other broad-based stock market index. For example, look at the late-2007/2008/early-2009 market downturn, and ask yourself honestly, "What if I had invested $100,000 on October 9, 2007 (peak of market) and saw my portfolio fall 55 percent (right before the bottom in early March 2009), what would I have done?"

The moderately aggressive or aggressive risk tolerances
If your answer is "invest more" to "buy low" then you may have what it takes to consider yourself an aggressive investor or maybe a moderately aggressive investor. Your focus is on growth, and you are willing

to accept large fluctuations in the value of your investments for the higher potential return that you might get by doing so.

The moderate risk tolerance

Again, reminding ourselves that hindsight is 20/20, and agreeing that we do not want to see the inevitable declines in our portfolio, the moderate investor looks at this same downturn and looks back and says, "I understand downturns happen and would have been willing to accept some (but not all) of this risk, say, a 15–25 percent downturn, for the potential upside that the portfolio may provide."

The conservative or moderately conservative risk tolerances

If your answer is "sell everything to end the pain" then you are *possibly* a conservative investor and may be as adventuresome as moderately conservative. Also referred to as "risk-averse," you are willing to tolerate little, if any, loss on the money you are investing. Your primary focus is principal protection and, secondary to this, income generation from your investments. The biggest challenge with this investment style/risk profile is finding investments that return enough to beat the rate of inflation.

So, did the first piece of the risk puzzle fit onto the second piece? In other words, did your score on the risk tolerance questionnaire match your response to the inflection point what-if test? If it did, we can move on to the next puzzle piece. If it did not, then you should go back to step one, the risk tolerance questionnaire, and try again, perhaps talking to your financial advisor about it or asking for guidance. However, don't do this right away . . . sleep on it. Hopefully, on the second time around with the risk questionnaire, your first and second puzzle pieces will fit together.

Before we move on to the third puzzle piece, let me make a point worth saying: No investor likes seeing his or her portfolio decrease, not even an *aggressive* investor. However, for the discerning investor, being even-keeled and logical (unemotional) will aid in making the decisions

> **Key Point:** *It is easy to be aggressive when markets are going up. Your true risk tolerance is tested when markets go down.*

that might, at the time, seem counterintuitive to a more conservative or undiscriminating investor. These investors will take advantage of the opportunity that inevitable downturns create.

The Third Puzzle Piece—The Upside vs. the Downside

How much you could lose is only half of the risk quotient. The other half that needs to be considered is *how much you could gain*. Obviously, the only reason to take on risk is to generate a return greater than a lower-risk asset, such as a certificate of deposit (CD), provides. So, in order to truly appreciate risk, you should consider not just the possibility of loss, but also the potential for a gain at various risk levels.

Take a look at Figure 6.5 for example. Let's suppose that A, B, C, D, and E represent a conservative, moderately conservative, moderate, moderately aggressive, and aggressive portfolios, respectively.

This exercise is not meant to be scientific. In fact, it is more of a "gut check" and confirmation than a mathematical question. The hypothetical situations in this chart allow you to visualize the fact that risk and return go hand in hand. The more incremental risk you take, the more potential return you might receive. Furthermore, you need to prepare yourself for the very good market conditions *and* the very bad market conditions.

So how do you use this information? You would simply ask yourself: What portfolio would I feel most comfortable with? For example, if your risk questionnaire suggests that you are a "moderate investor," take a look at Portfolio C. Would you feel comfortable knowing that with 95 percent confidence, this portfolio, historically, would have had returns ranging from 33.79 percent to −13.65 percent and an average of 10.07 percent? You need to remember a couple key points when you complete this exercise. First, past performance is not indicative of future results. This consideration pertains to this chart *or* any investment you might make. Second, and it is worth repeating, this exercise is not meant to be a mathematical equation. Instead, it is meant to show you that if you take risk (downside) you *could* be compensated with an attractive return, and that return is

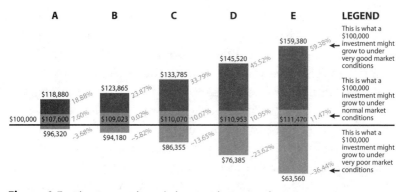

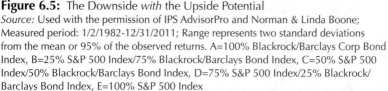

Figure 6.5: The Downside *with* the Upside Potential
Source: Used with the permission of IPS AdvisorPro and Norman & Linda Boone; Measured period: 1/2/1982-12/31/2011; Range represents two standard deviations from the mean or 95% of the observed returns. A=100% Blackrock/Barclays Corp Bond Index, B=25% S&P 500 Index/75% Blackrock/Barclays Bond Index, C=50% S&P 500 Index/50% Blackrock/Barclays Bond Index, D=75% S&P 500 Index/25% Blackrock/Barclays Bond Index, E=100% S&P 500 Index

likely to be higher with additional risk. With regard to this second point, if your risk questionnaire suggests that you are moderately aggressive, yet you might be willing to be aggressive, you need to ask yourself: "For the *potential* additional return of 13.86 percent (59.38% − 45.52%), would I be willing to take the additional *potential* hit of a 12.82 percent loss (36.44% − 23.62%)?" Remember, this assessment represents 95 percent of the observed returns over this period of time, and you would have a 5 percent chance of higher or lower returns.

The Fourth Puzzle Piece—Probability of a Loss

Let's suppose that you build an investment portfolio that you believe matches your risk tolerance. Now you will want to confirm, using historical data, that the portfolio will not be more volatile than you expect it to be. Ask yourself this question: "What are the chances I can lose (or gain) more than *X* percent with this portfolio?" As we venture into puzzle piece four, please note that this material may be more information than you need in order to have a high degree of confidence in your portfolio and its associated risk. If you start reading this chapter and find yourself "tuning out" with a "deer in the headlights look," then simply skip puzzle piece four. Think of this section as "advanced risk assessment."

Again, the goal of these four puzzle pieces is to help you confirm that the risk level you take matches your tolerance for risk and, therefore, can help give you confidence and conviction to enjoy the good times, but also to "hang in there" for the tough markets. Also, please remember that past performance does not indicate future results. The data you will be using in this formula relate to the portfolio's *historical returns and risk*. Even though they may not be indicative of the future, they are the only data we have for the portfolio and, therefore, will serve as a general guide.

So how do you determine the probability of a certain loss (or gain) in your portfolio?

Step One: Gather your "data":

After you build your investment portfolio, you will need its *standard deviation* and *mean return*. I suggest using the longest data available for the entire portfolio. For example, if all the investments have a 10-year track record, you should use these data instead of the 3-year data.

This information is widely available from fund companies, research firms, such as Morningstar®, and of course your financial advisor, if you work with one.

Step 2: Input the data into the formula:

$$z = \frac{x - \mu}{\sigma}.$$

Technically speaking, z is the deviation of x away from the mean, μ, $(x - \mu)$ expressed as the number of standard deviations, σ. However, unless you are a mathematician or just someone who likes statistics, you don't need to try to memorize or analyze this formula for a test. The easier way to understand this concept is to use an example to illustrate its use.

Example: If you were concerned about the probability of losing more than 22 percent of your investment, you would begin by calculating the number of standard deviations that –22 percent is away from your expected return. Let's say your expected return is 8 percent and the standard deviation of your portfolio is 15 percent. Then you would calculate:

$$z = (-22 - 8)/15 = -2.$$

The loss you're concerned about is two standard deviations[37] below the mean.

Note: For those less-technical readers, you don't have to worry about understanding the definition of standard deviation or that this calculation determines how many standard deviations away from the mean you have calculated. The focus should simply be inputting the numbers correctly—standard deviation, mean, and the measurement you are looking for (i.e., chance of losing more than 22%), then calculating the answer (i.e., do the math), and moving on to Step 3 to determine your answer.

Step 3: Use a Standard Normal Distribution table to calculate the chances:

Sample Probabilities: Probability of Earning a Return That Is Less Than Shown	
z	Probability
–3	0.14%
–2	2.3%
–1	15.9%
0	50%
1	84%
2	98%
3	99.9%

---

[37] Standard deviation is a statistical measurement that sheds light on historical volatility. It is the dispersion of a set of returns from its mean. It shows the spread of an investment's returns (positive and negative) over time and is commonly used to gauge potential volatility or risk. The greater the degree of dispersion, the greater the risk. For example, a volatile stock will have a high standard deviation while the deviation of a stable blue chip stock will be lower.

Locate −2 in the *z* column. From there, you can see a 2.3 percent chance of a loss of 22 percent or more. (More technically speaking, the 2.3% chance of losing 22% or more is due to the fact that −22% is −2 standard deviations [15%] away from the 8% mean.)

Let's look at a few hypothetical examples to solidify your understanding.

Example 1:   Suppose you have a portfolio of ten mutual funds that have a 10-year mean return[38] of 7 percent and a standard deviation of 12 percent. You want to know the probability of *gaining at least* 8 percent on this portfolio (based on historical data). Note: Because we are determining the probability of a *gain,* we take one additional step (see Step 4). Again, you can determine the mean return and standard deviation from your financial advisor or through a research firm such as Morningstar.®

Step 1: Gather your data:

Mean = μ = 7%

Standard deviation = σ = 12%

Measurement you want to calculate = *x* = Probability of *gaining at least* 8%

Step 2: Input the data into the formula:

$z = 8 − 7/12 = 0.08$

Subtract 7 from 8, and then divide the answer by 12.

Step 3: Use the Standard Normal Distribution Table (found in Appendix 6-B) to calculate your chances of earning at least 8 percent.
   a) Find 0.0 under the *z* column.
   b) Move to right and find .08. Please note that the columns (.01, .02, etc.) provide more precision in your table lookup.

---

[38] A mean (geometric) return is also called the time-weighted rate of return, a measure of the compound rate of growth of the initial portfolio market value during the evaluation period, assuming that all cash distributions are reinvested in the portfolio. It is computed by taking the geometric average of the portfolio subperiod returns.

You will see 0.53188.

Step 4: (This additional step is only needed when determining the probability of a gain**).**

Subtract the number from Step 3 from "1":

$1 - 0.53188 = 0.46812$

You would have a 46.81 percent chance of *gaining more than* 8 percent with this portfolio.

Example 2: Let's suppose you have a portfolio that includes five exchange-traded funds and three mutual funds. With the help of your financial advisor or a research firm (such as Morningstar®), you determine that the overall portfolio had a mean return of 5 percent and a standard deviation of 10 percent. You want to know what is the probability of losing more than 30 percent.

Step 1: Gather your data:

Mean $= \mu = 5\%$

Standard Deviation $= \sigma = 10\%$

Measurement you want to calculate $= x =$ Probability of *losing more than* 30%

Step 2: Input the data into the formula:

$z = (-30 - 5)/10 = -3.5$

Subtract 5 from −30, and then divide the answer by 10.

Step 3: Use the Standard Normal Distribution Table (found in Appendix 6-B) to calculate your chances of losing more than 30 percent:

a) Find -3.5 under the z column.
b) Move to right and find .00.

You will see 0.00023. You have a 0.023 percent (very unlikely) chance of *losing more than* 30 percent.

ADD SOME PERSPECTIVE TO YOUR PUZZLE

Now you have four puzzle pieces that fit together and hopefully a good understanding of the risk that you are willing to take. Although we have all heard the saying, "Past performance is not indicative of future results," I am repeating it for a good reason. It does help us if we really listen to the meaning of this statement. Future gains will not necessarily be similar to past gains; however, they can give us some *perspective*. In Chapter 1, we learned that having perspective of the importance of money is essential. Well, perspective is equally important as it relates to your experience with investing and risk. Understanding and appreciating how you have reacted in the past to both good *and* bad markets can sometimes teach good lessons. In other words, learn from your experiences.

I am the father of three great kids. As a parent, I get to observe my children having experiences similar to those that other children have—playing sports, working hard for good grades, the pressures of peers, and so on. Watching "the thrill of victory and the agony of defeat" during kids' sports is sometimes an emotional roller coaster for both children *and* parents alike. My son, Nick (who is 10 at this time), was playing a football game recently for his team, the Elkridge Hurricanes. It was a hard-fought game that eventually led to overtime. In overtime, Nick's team had four downs from the 10-yard line to score a touchdown. Unfortunately, they were unable to score, which gave the other team a chance to win (if neither team scored, it would go down as a tie). So, as Nick took the field on defense, he knew the best outcome would be a tie . . . if they could prevent a touchdown. The opposing team ran the ball on first down and the ball carrier was running full speed toward Nick from the 10-yard line. Nick was the only player between the ball carrier and the end zone. My heart was pounding as if I was in the game. Unfortunately, he missed the tackle and the other team scored. After the game he was crying and felt miserable. Later in the day, we talked about that final play. He knew he missed an opportunity, but he also knew that the next time he was faced with this situation, he would learn from what happened and be better prepared to make the play. It was a tough, but important, learning experience for Nick.

My view is this: If the first time you do something and it does not work out as planned, it is a learning experience. If you do the same thing again and have the same undesired result, it is a mistake. And doing the same thing over and over again and expecting different results, well . . . that's just insanity. (This statement has been attributed to Albert Einstein.) I believe I mentioned my view about this in Chapter 2, but I feel it bears repeating.

Before we move on, I should point out that some investors will, in fact, bear lower risk (i.e., by investing *only* in certificates of deposits [CDs] or Treasury securities). We are purposely not including this investor in our conversation. Although this investor has the potential to enjoy steady returns, he or she will incur a different type of risk: purchasing power risk (risk of loss in the value of cash due to inflation). Although this investing style/risk level falls outside of this discussion, suffice it to say that investors who bear lower (market) risk need to appreciate that they may not be able to keep up with inflation over time.

The goal of these exercises and working with the puzzle pieces is to help give you confidence. You must have conviction to invest. Without it, you cannot successfully get through the tough times in the market. It's easier to invest when markets are running smoothly, but when they are uncertain, your confidence can be drastically tested. You need to be able to have the confidence that your investment strategies are based on sound principles, and that the entire world economy is not going to collapse (even though the media noise might make you think it will).

RISK EVOLVES AS WE AGE, SOMETIMES

Conventional wisdom tells us what to do when we are younger: "Pay yourself first" by saving regularly, based on the amount determined in your financial plan. Invest it as aggressively as your risk tolerance allows on the principle that, over the long run, more investment risk should lead to more investment reward. But once we get into our fifties and sixties and beyond, the "long run" isn't as long as it used to be. In fact, as we reach "retirement" age, it may be only a few years before we need to start withdrawing from our saved or invested assets for retirement income.

Does that mean you should flip the switch and become conservative? My answer would be "not necessarily." Because people are living longer these days, and because inflation reduces purchasing power, our investments need to grow if we are going to maintain our living standard over an extended period of time. In most cases, what is prudent might be to "drift" slowly toward a more conservative portfolio. For example, in your sixties you may have a moderate or moderately conservative risk level. Then, in your seventies you reduce it to moderately conservative or conservative. When you are in your eighties or nineties, you switch to conservative (with possibly a substantial percentage of assets in traditionally "safer" investments like Treasuries). Preferably, the best time to make these gradual shifts is after you have experienced a solid gain in your account(s).

I can think of one scenario in which you would throw out conventional wisdom (drifting toward a more conservative portfolio over time). After careful planning, you determine that with your lifestyle, income sources, expense estimates, and inflation assumptions, you will have enough income to live on without using your investments— either entirely or partially. In this case, you may plan on passing to younger heirs the wealth you have determined you will not need for your lifetime.

For instance, let's suppose that you are in your seventies, have a pension, and are collecting Social Security benefits, both with the potential for cost-of-living adjustments. You have adequate long-term care and health insurance. You are living comfortably, well within your income, and you have a substantial portfolio. In this case, you may determine that you will not need to use this money during your lifetime and it could, therefore, be invested for the benefit of your children or other younger heirs. For this reason, you may want to consider investing with their risk tolerance, not yours. Just be careful with this strategy: When the market is inevitably in one of its downward cycles, you may need to remind yourself of the strategy and repeat after me: "I am investing for the next generation, I am investing for the next generation, I am investing for the next generation. . . ." Repeat this mantra as needed.

GETTING IT RIGHT THE FIRST TIME

Do you remember the story about Goldilocks and the three bears? Goldilocks was hungry and tasted from the three bowls of porridge until she found the one that was "just right." Well, investing is oddly similar. If you don't get your risk tolerance right, investing might be "too cold" or "too hot" and leave a bad taste in your mouth.

For example, if you are too conservative (in bull markets), your portfolio may not keep up with the general equities market, and you may try to increase your risk (more equities) just at the wrong time ... *after the market has increased.* Remember, the name of the game is "buy low, sell high," not the other way around. If you let emotions enter the decision-making process, you may do the opposite and buy high or sell low. Remember to reflect on your risk tolerance and to review your risk profile. Read your questionnaire and your answers to help you maintain the same attitudes, thoughts, and viewpoints on risk.

THE RISK OF MARKET TIMING

This chapter would not be complete without a few words on the strategy (and risk) of market timing. Market timing is the method of making buy or sell decisions about stocks by attempting to predict future market price movements. The prediction may be based on an outlook of the market or economic conditions as a result of technical or fundamental analysis. You may get lucky now and then, but market timing is a hard strategy to pull off consistently enough to make good returns. It is generally agreed that investors have poor timing, becoming less risk-averse when markets are high and more risk-averse when markets are low.

The problem is that humans are not entirely rational beings. The proponents of behavioral finance claim that investors are irrational, but their biases are consistent and predictable. Evidence against market timing is clear in the famous study[39] by Dalbar (the nation's leading financial-services market research firm), which found that the average investor's return in stocks is much less than the amount that

---

[39] *www.dalbar.com*

would have been obtained by simply holding an index fund consisting of all stocks contained in the S&P 500 index. The evidence of these results can be found in Figure 6.6. As you see, the average investor, because of the timing of their investments, has not done as well as the

The Average Investor Underperforms
20-Year Annualized Returns by Asset Class (1992–2011)

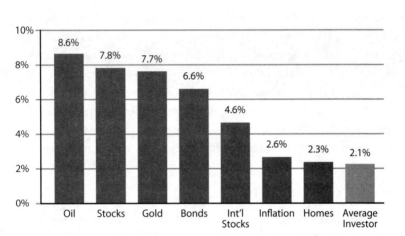

Figure 6.6: The 20-Year Return (1992–2011) for the Average Investor is Abysmal
Source: BlackRock; Bloomberg; Informa Investment Solutions; Dalbar. Past performance is no guarantee of future results. It is not possible to directly invest in an index. Oil is represented by the NYMEX Light Sweet Crude Future Index. Contract size is 1,000 barrels with a contract price quoted in US Dollars and Cents per barrel. Delivery dates take place every month of the year. Gold is represented by the change in the spot price of gold in USD per ounce. Homes are represented by the Existing One Family Home Sales Median Price Index. Stocks are represented by the S&P 500 Index, an unmanaged index that consists of the common stocks of 500 large-capitalization companies, within various industrial sectors, most of which are listed on the New York Stock Exchange. Bonds are represented by the Barclays Capital US Aggregate Bond Index, an unmanaged market-weighted index that consists of investment-grade corporate bonds (rated BBB or better), mortgages and US Treasury and government agency issues with at least 1 year to maturity. International Stocks are represented by the MSCI EAFE Index, a broad-based measure of international stock performance. Inflation is represented by the Consumer Price Index. Average Investor is represented by Dalbar's average asset allocation investor return, which utilizes the net of aggregate mutual fund sales, redemptions and exchanges each month as a measure of investor behavior. Returns are annualized (and total return where applicable) and represent the 20-year period ending 12/31/11 to match Dalbar's most recent analysis.

general markets. Lou Harvey, the president of Dalbar, was quoted as saying, "This finding is consistent with the well-known behavior of investors to brag about their gains but remain silent about losses. The occasional money makers create the illusion that all market timers are winners all the time. The fact is that most timers lose money most often and this data now confirms it." Case in point: the most notorious market timer in our industry, Joe Granville, who made it big with some wild hits during the waning President Carter years, has not had any market timing wins in decades. According to the *Hulbert Financial Digest*'s rankings, "'The Granville Market Letter' is at the bottom for performance during the past 25 years, having produced average losses of more than 20 percent per year on an annualized basis."

> **Key Point:** *Hindsight is 20/20.*

At this stage, if you still think you have a special gift for knowing when to get out of the market, and, more importantly, when to get back into the market, please take a cue from some of these famous investors. They may give you pause to reconsider:

Warren Buffett, legendary value investor

"The only value of stock forecasters is to make fortune-tellers look good."

"I never attempt to make money on the stock market. I buy on the assumption that they could close the market the next day and not reopen it for five years."

"Stop trying to predict the direction of the stock market, the economy, interest rates, or elections."

"Much success can be attributed to inactivity. Most investors cannot resist the temptation to constantly buy and sell."

"Success in investing doesn't correlate with I.Q. once you're above the level of 25. Once you have ordinary intelligence, what you need is the temperament to control the urges that get other people into trouble in investing."

Peter Lynch, renowned investor and former head of Fidelity Magellan

> "Far more money has been lost by investors preparing for corrections, or trying to anticipate corrections, than has been lost in corrections themselves."

> "I can't recall ever once having seen the name of a market timer on *Forbes'* annual list of the richest people in the world. If it were truly possible to predict corrections, you'd think somebody would have made billions by doing it."

Jason Zweig, personal finance columnist for *The Wall Street Journal*

> "Whenever some analyst seems to know what he's talking about, remember that pigs will fly before he'll ever release a full list of his past forecasts, including the bloopers."

Jonathan Clements, Director of Financial Education for Citi Personal Wealth Management

> "What to do when the market goes down? Read the opinions of the investment gurus who are quoted in the *WSJ*. And, as you read, laugh. We all know that the pundits can't predict short-term market movements. Yet there they are, desperately trying to sound intelligent when they really haven't got a clue."

Fortune Magazine

> "Let's say it clearly: No one knows where the market is going—experts or novices, soothsayers or astrologers. That's the simple truth."

The Wall Street Journal

> "A decade of results throws cold water on the notion that strategists exhibit any special ability to time the markets."

IN CLOSING

Risk analysis is a dynamic process, not a static event; the types of risk, sources of risk, and your risk tolerance will react to our ever-changing world. Portfolio performance is comprised of both risk and return, but the first step in investment management is to determine your risk tolerance—a combination of subjective and quantitative analysis—to help you determine how much volatility you can emotionally handle. Although no single test (like an X-ray that determines whether you have a broken bone) can determine a person's risk tolerance, we use a combination of questions and various scenarios to assist us. We call it our "risk puzzle" and it includes four pieces that should fit together in order for you to view the overall picture of your investment risk. The first puzzle piece is "the Questionnaire," which helps you determine the level of risk you are willing to take and indicates whether you are a conservative, moderately conservative, moderate, moderately aggressive, or aggressive investor.

The second piece of the puzzle is the "Pain Threshold Test," which prepares you for the real world. We looked at various investment scenarios with the help of the inflection points and asked ourselves what-if scenarios (with the benefit of hindsight) that can show you how much risk you are willing to take, if any. The third puzzle piece, "the Upside vs. the Downside," reminded us to look at the potential reward relative to each risk level. Finally, with the fourth puzzle piece, "the Probability Test," we determined how to calculate the probability of losing money in your portfolio.

It's also worth repeating that market timing, when trying to avoid risk, doesn't work well, and we've given you a few examples of why it doesn't. Of course, you could get lucky every now and then, but it is an especially difficult strategy to employ on a reliable basis to bring in good returns.

The goal of this chapter is to help educate you in the area of risk and to provide tools to help give you the confidence and conviction you need to invest with self-assurance. We truly believe it takes patience to invest. I like to call it the "art" of patience. Art cannot be rushed, and patience cannot be lost if the "painting" is to be finished.

Let's use the fresco technique as an example. Michelangelo's magnificent fresco on the Sistine Chapel's ceiling was a labor of love. It required a significant amount of patience and the process took skill, as well as significant time. To explain the process a bit, a fresco is a type of mural painting executed on plaster walls, ceilings, or any other type of flat surface. It is impervious to decay, delaminating, or fading, and the only element that can demise its beauty is either erosion or physical chipping away at the surface. Specifically, Michelangelo used a wash technique to apply broad areas of color; then as the surface became drier, he revisited these areas with a more linear approach, adding shade and detail with a variety of brushes. He employed all the finest workshop methods and best innovations, combining them with a diversity of brushwork and breadth of skill far exceeding those of the best painters of the time. You must have a long-term dedication to the fresco mural before you actually begin to paint. Not only must the artist possess a vision and love for long-term projects, he or she must have a goal in mind, a strong intellect, a good measure of patience, masterful painting skills, and a good dose of strength (mentally and physically). There are also many other critical components that require long-term dedication to the mural before the process even begins.

This is similar to the critical components that are so important to understand regarding risk and your risk capacity before you begin an investment program—one you will be proud to call your masterpiece.

7 | Preparing the "Mixture"

"If you knew how much work went into it, you wouldn't call it genius."

—Michelangelo

A PAINTER'S COLOR MIXTURE, AS WELL AS THE TYPE OF APPLICATION USED, such as Michelangelo's fresco technique and its imperviousness to decay and fading, could mean the difference between a painting that is displayed in a museum for generations to come or one that ends up in the curator's storage closet. While a painter uses his or her artistic vision to mix colors on a palette and decides which application to use, an investor needs more substance than just an artistic vision to create an investment masterpiece—a sustainable portfolio.

So, how do investors use their palette—covered with investments of various risk—to narrow down the number of choices and create an "investment mixture" that meets their requirements for risk and return? The choice, allocation, and timing of purchases and sales of investments are typically based on analysis or theory and once in a while, a gut feeling. But which one and why? Do you stick with the buy-and-hold strategy even when the markets are going down? What investment traits do you have to consider? How much of a role do the current economic conditions play in your investment choices?

As you might guess, many interdependent variables factor into the question: How do we find the right "mixture" of investments?

The purpose of this chapter, along with support from Chapters 6 and 8, is to help you build a resilient portfolio with the hope it can weather the ups and downs that are an inevitable part of investing. After your risk tolerance is determined (Chapter 6), you can focus on the next decision: How do you invest your retirement nest egg so that you don't take too much risk *or* too little risk? The answer for many readers: you allocate your portfolio based on a model that was suggested to you by your financial advisor, a financial magazine, or a website. Others may be using technical analysis or some other methodology to tactically shift their portfolio from different asset classes (i.e., U.S. stocks, foreign bonds, etc.). Although I believe technical analysis and tactical management may play a role, I also believe these concepts will function only in a minor way in your investment mixture. At the core, your portfolio should be designed with a diversified mixture of investments.

In this chapter you will learn about diversification. We will review the definition as well as past theories and strategies that formed current popular beliefs and investment philosophies. However, my goal in this chapter is for you to finish reading it and realize that you might not want to stay with the status quo. I hope you question your strategy and come to the conclusion that you are either still comfortable (and you have conviction) with your current investment strategy, *or* you determine that a further and thorough review is appropriate in light of what you've learned.

As we delve into this chapter, please understand I will mention technical terms at times. I will attempt to simplify the terminology through the use of examples and analogies. If, after reading the material, you still have difficulty grasping the entire concept, don't worry. Try to appreciate the fundamental concept and move on. Although it would be nice, you will not become an investment genius for your friends to envy after reading this book. However, I'm hopeful it will help you become more educated about the key ingredients that might help you implement a successful investment portfolio and live a fulfilled life.

In the next chapter, we will build on this topic and discuss specific types of investments that may be suitable to help you achieve those goals.

WHAT IS DIVERSIFICATION?

Diversify. Diversify. Diversify. This has been the mantra and the advice preached to investors for decades and followed by most financial advisors, mutual fund companies, endowments, financial media, and corporations. We all know it is important, but what does it really mean? In the midst of the theories and the technical definitions, if you ask various people (advisors, investors, endowments, etc.), you will get various answers. Think about this:

> *If you ask 100 financial advisors how to diversify the nest egg of a recent retiree in his or her mid-sixties with "moderate" risk (all else being the same), you would likely get 100 different answers—variations of different types of investments, asset classes, products, and strategies. The point being, while there is a science to diversification, much of it is just subjective interpretation of numerous theories, calculations, ideas, and so on. Diversification in and of itself is a mixture of art and science.*

Clearly, the definition of diversification is partially personal. Building an investment portfolio, at least for me, is like choosing a tie at the clothing store. With so many alternatives on the display tables—colors, patterns, themes, and designs—the choice is almost endless. It boils down to a personal preference. So if you ask yourself or a financial expert, "How much of my portfolio should be invested in U.S. stocks?" and "What stocks are best?" you also have to ask yourself the question, "How are the answers determined?" The answer: personal preference. While this "preference" may not be subjective like art—it may be based on formulas, calculations and theories—it is still the individual's interpretation of those measures and concepts that determines the ultimate investment chosen.

When it comes to diversification, I have heard and seen it all. When asking 401(k) participants how they diversify, I sometimes receive responses ranging from, "I pick the ones that have performed the best over the past three years," to "Oh, my employer or fund company [holding the securities] handles that." Of course, picking investments that have done well in the past does not necessarily mean they will do well in the future. In fact, most investments are cyclical in nature, and this strategy may possibly set the investor up for failure. Furthermore, employers and fund companies that act as a custodian for plans do not typically give advice on which specific investment to use. I have seen prospective clients who have their entire portfolio in U.S. large cap stock funds with similar holdings and styles. While this approach may provide potential exposure to more stocks, it is possible that the underlying companies in the mutual funds are the same and, therefore, might act with similar price movements. Most often, no real benefit comes from having the same stocks in different investments.

A seemingly unlimited array of books, articles, theories, opinions, noise, and Nobel Prize Laureates all discuss the subject of diversification. To name a few:

- In 1949, the famous value investor and mentor to Warren Buffett, Benjamin Graham, in his book *The Intelligent Investor*, suggested that adequate diversification can be obtained with 10 to 30 stocks.

- In 1968, in an article in the *Journal of Finance*, authors Evans and Archer concluded that having only 10 stocks in your portfolio would give you the same risk, as measured by standard deviation, as the entire market.

- Or, take the strategy in the book *A Random Walk Down Wall Street,* first published in 1973. It suggests that a portfolio of 20 equal-sized stocks and well-diversified issues would reduce risk by about 70 percent. Furthermore, if you add more stocks to the basket (beyond 20), you would not reduce risk significantly.

- Another theory of diversification is explained in the widely touted 1986 study, "Determinants of Portfolio Performance" by Gary P. Brinson, L. Randolph Hood, and Gilbert L. Beebower. They stated that 93 percent of the variability of returns are explained by asset allocation,[40] which is the combination of more than one type

---

[40] Asset allocation programs do not assure a profit or protect against loss in declining markets. No program can guarantee that any objective or goal will be achieved.

of asset class (i.e., large U.S. stocks) that produces a better risk-adjusted return than the individual investments on their own.

• Or take the popular, time-honored, "60/40" portfolio, which consists of 60 percent stocks and 40 percent bonds. The media and many well-known and respected financial services companies would have you consider this allocation as appropriate for your retirement years. Sometimes called "balanced" or "moderate," this allocation (60% S&P 500 and 40% Barclays Aggregate Bond Index) would have lost 30.3 percent in the 2008 financial crisis (October 9, 2007–March 9, 2009)! According to the 2012 Natixis Global Asset Management U.S. Advisor survey, an estimated 49 percent of advisors queried say they're "uncertain that the traditional 60/40 allocation between stocks and bonds is still the strategy to take." Furthermore, according to the same study, an estimated 40 percent of advisors with 15-plus years of experience believe that a 60/40 stock and bond mix is not the best strategy to seek returns and manage risk.

I can't leave this section without mentioning a classic rule of thumb—the good ol' "take your age and subtract it from 100" approach. The answer to this equation is the amount you should invest in equities. Back in the late 1990s, as the market was frothing with technology stocks and everybody thought they were aggressive because "stocks could only go up," the number changed to 110 minus your age, which made the portfolios more heavily invested in equities. Although this rule of thumb is just that—a rule of thumb—it was easy to understand and, therefore, was quite popular among many investors, including the growing do-it-yourself investors.

Many of these theories were derived from modern portfolio theory (MPT). Modern portfolio theory, first publicized in the 1950s by Nobel prize-winning economist Harry Markowitz, is based on the idea that not all investments move in the same direction at the same time; some may increase in value (zig) when others decrease in value (zag). Correlation, which we will discuss in more detail later in the chapter, is a measure of the direction you can expect one investment in your portfolio to change in price, relative to another. For instance, the price of steel might go up, which is great for the steel industry but bad for the auto industry because carmakers will have to pay more for materials. As a result, you could expect investments in these two areas to move in opposite directions. These investments have a negative correlation. In contrast, one might expect an investment in the tire industry to closely track investments in the automobile industry, which is a positive correlation. Modern portfolio theory contends that a portfolio's performance can be improved by diversification, which means selecting investments that are noncorrelated to one another. Note that diversification alone cannot guarantee a profit or protect your portfolio from losing value, but the concept can create a foundation on which to build your investment portfolio.

Even though I have only scratched the surface, you can begin to see that the theories on asset allocation and diversification could fill many books, articles, and magazines (and indeed they already have!). I would suggest that most, if not all, of the previously mentioned theories, as well as many others, stand on solid research using data *that were available at that time.* Since the time period during which each of these studies has been presented, follow-up data suggest some of them are still valid and valuable. With that said, a number of studies have tried to debunk them, some of which are quite convincing. For example, the research of Brinson, Hood, and Beebower was not about total return. It was about *volatility.* Yet, investors assumed that asset allocation influences long-term return as much as it influences volatility. And as the critics noted, volatility and return may be related, but they're two different things.

> **Key Point:** *Diversification strategies evolve over time; what was considered prudent at one time may be different now.*

In my opinion, investors unfortunately have relied too heavily on these strategies without having the flexibility to adapt to the changing world economies. Consider this: Is it possible, after all the world has experienced with wars, recessions, tax code changes, new technologies, new products, and such, that an investment theory developed 60 years ago still is valid today? How about 30 years ago?

My conclusion is as follows:

Many of these past studies and theories are still valuable from a holistic perspective and to appreciate, but they need to be further adapted to today's environment. Additionally, investors need to have flexibility to make changes to their diversification strategy as new products are created and as the economies of the world evolve. More and more ideas will be suggested on how to diversify properly, but, as we know, it is vital to separate the noise from the proven, time-tested strategies. We will talk more about the need for this flexibility in the next few pages of the book.

Simply put, diversification is used in portfolios to help reduce volatility, to help you get from Point A in time to Point B, with less risk. If you aren't worried about the ups and downs of your portfolio and are willing to take an unlimited amount of risk, you might not need to diversify. However, if you are like most investors, this approach would cause you too much heartburn and stress.

So the question we should periodically ask ourselves: "Is the strategy I am using to diversify still sound?" Remember, if you are taking risk, you could lose the value of your investments, but that does not equate to an unsound strategy. Let's take a few moments for perspective, to look back in time and see the investment world for what it has *been*.

IT IS DIFFERENT "THIS TIME"

Throughout 2008 and the beginning of 2009, I was constantly reminded from clients, friends, news media, and just about everyone I spoke to, that *this downturn* was different. Yes, it was different. The next downturn will be different, too. You see, every bear market is different, just like every bull market, expansion, and recession is different. And guess what? When you are in it, it almost always *feels* more painful than the last one.

Our past has been fraught with problems: scandals, bubbles, natural disasters, wars, acts of terrorism, political gridlock, company failures, trading mistakes, and flash crashes. We will never know what is going to come at us next. What we *do* know is that we cannot control most of these problems, and that they will continue to happen. I suspect that they will not only continue to happen, but will happen more frequently and with more impact to market returns due to the ever-increasing complexity of the world. They are the types of things we can't control. What we can control is our *expectations* when these events happen in the future.

Many investors don't appreciate the timing of returns. Some expect that if they are moderate investors with say, a goal of 6 percent per year, they should earn returns close to 6 percent each year. However, the reality is that returns can be much higher or lower than the average. Of course, the riskier the portfolio, the more variation from this average is possible. For example, take a look at Figure 7.1, which shows quite a lot of returns outside of the 0–10 percent range, the range that most investors expect to earn. While diversification may help reduce the extreme returns (−30% to −50%), diversification alone cannot protect you completely. Make sure that you have reasonable expectations of what diversification can and can't do for your portfolio.

At this point in the chapter, we have a basic understanding of the following:

- Many different definitions of diversification and theories on investments are floating around out there. And the future undoubtedly holds many more. Although most have substance and logic behind the "math," we live in a world that is constantly changing and you may need to look at variations and multiple theories and strategies to adequately diversify.

- Numerous events in the world have caused panic in the markets, which will continue to be the case. Due to the complexity of our society and increasing sophistication of technology, I believe these events will happen with an ever-increasing frequency and a more impactful effect to markets.

- Even though we might believe we have a well-diversified portfolio, the markets don't always stay in a comfortable range. They

S&P Index from 1825 to 2012

Positive years: 131 (70%)
Negative years: 57 (30%)

Percentage Total Return

Figure 7.1: Be Ready for Anything
Source: Value Square Asset Management, Yale University, http://icf.som.yale.edu/
old-new-york-stock-exchange-1815-1925

will always have their outliers (very high or very low returns) in some years, even with a "diversified portfolio."

- The main reason to diversify is to attempt to reduce the volatility of your portfolio.

IT HAS WORKED IN THE PAST. WILL IT WORK IN THE FUTURE?

Most readers will agree that diversification is an important part of managing risk. The question then becomes, "Can we rely on the same diversification strategies we have used in the past?" The answer will be revealed in the next few pages.

At the time of this writing, I am outlining some of the main reasons that we need to consider changing the way we currently diversify. You may be reading this book possibly years or decades after it was written, so the list may be different. The list itself is not the message here. The message is that we need to be aware that times change, and with changing times comes the need to be flexible and to have the ability to change diversification strategies. Following are the six reasons why we may need to change the way we diversify our portfolios.

> **Key Point:** *We need to walk a fine line where, on one side, we have the needed conviction to believe in our diversification strategy(s) and, on the other side of that fine line, know when those strategies need to be changed to adapt to new information and products.*

SIX REASONS WHY WE NEED TO CHANGE THE WAY WE DIVERSIFY

As we read in the preceding paragraphs, diversification methods and theories change over time. I believe we need to consider six factors as we adapt our diversification strategy. They include issues that are relevant as this book is written as well as factors that will continue for possibly decades into the future.

Trends That May Continue	Our Current and Near-Term Future
Correlations are increasing.	Interest rates are low.
Volatility is increasing.	Government/sovereign involvement is increasing.
Scammers, scandals, and mistrust are increasing.	Deleveraging may be a painful process.

1. It Is Tougher to Find Noncorrelated Investments

Although I promised that I would try to keep to a minimum the technical jargon and financial lingo, I am going to discuss a concept that may be somewhat new to some readers of this book. That concept is "correlation."

By the way, when people talk about stuff that I don't understand and they can't relate it to me in a way that I can comprehend, I get frustrated. I sometimes "tune out." My friend Lou did this to me the other day. Lou owns an alarm installation and monitoring company. He is branching out with a cutting-edge technology that uses radio frequency to build a network infrastructure. We were on the phone for more than 30 minutes as he told me about this opportunity. I could tell he was excited and it was going to be lucrative. I listened to him carefully, trying to understand the key points and how it worked. I asked questions periodically to try to gain a better understanding. However, in the end, I had no idea what Lou was talking about. Finally, Lou said, "Just go to the Internet and Google it." My mechanic is another person who does the same thing to me. Actually, in an odd way, I think he enjoys it. I say to myself, "How can someone sit there and talk to me in all of these automotive terms, seeing that I have the 'deer in the headlights' look on my face?" I hope you don't tune out as we discuss this important concept.

My goal is to explain this and other subjects in the book that may be unfamiliar, but in a way that accomplishes two things:

- For those who know the subject matter, I want to confirm your knowledge and possibly refresh your understanding without boring you.

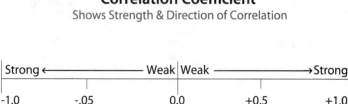

Correlation Coefficient
Shows Strength & Direction of Correlation

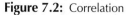

Figure 7.2: Correlation
Source: Williams Asset Management

- For those who are new to the subject matter, I want you to read this and say, "I understand the premise of what Gary is trying to say," without being bored.

Personally, I like to get to the core of stuff and find out the basic premise and meaning of things. When you try to drill down with the concept of diversification, the conversation can lead to tangents: asset allocation, buy-and-hold strategies, technical analysis, and many others. I would argue that when you "peel back the onion" to the core on this subject, you get to one word—correlation. More precisely, diversification equals noncorrelating assets. Before we go further, let's take a moment and give a technical definition of correlation: Correlation is the mutual relationship or connection between two or more things.

Don't let Figure 7.2 scare you. It is simple: correlation always has a range of +1 to −1. Correlation is a relationship between two quantities, such that when one changes, the other changes too. If the quantities simultaneously increase or decrease in value, a positive correlation exists. If one increases as the other decreases, a negative correlation exists. For example, the resale value of an automobile and its mileage tend to be negatively correlated; the more miles on a car's odometer, the less the car is worth. In contrast, auto insurance costs and accident incidents are positively correlated; the more accidents a driver experiences, the more costly the driver's auto insurance. See Figure 7.3.

Correlation
Relationship Between Two Quantities
Such That When One Changes, the Other Does

| Negative | Zero | Positive |

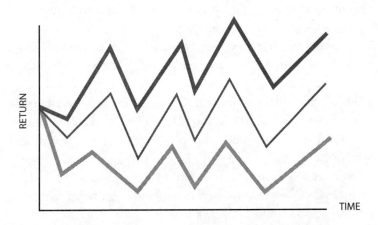

Figure 7.3: Example of Positive, Negative, and
Noncorrelated Relationships
Source: Williams Asset Management

Furthermore and sometimes misunderstood, having a positive correlation does not necessarily mean two investments move *exactly in tandem*. See Figure 7.4.

3 Assets with High Correlation Deliver Range of Returns

Note: Highly correlated assets can still provide diversification, defined as different returns. Concern is more with end result than with the pattern of gains & losses. Low correlation smooths out the ride. Cumulative stability is the objective.

Figure 7.4: Three Investments with High Correlation
Source: PPCA Inc.

Taking it one step further, strong correlation is typically considered any number over 0.75, while moderate correlation is between 0.25 and 0.75, and low correlation (which is what we strive for with diversification) would be between −0.25 and 0.25. According to the book mentioned earlier in the chapter, *A Random Walk Down Wall Street,* author and economist, Burton Malkiel, suggests:

- a correlation of +1.0 would result in no reduction of risk,
- a correlation of 0.50 would provide a moderate reduction of risk,
- a correlation of 0 would provide considerable risk reduction,
- a correlation of −0.50 can reduce most risk, and
- a correlation of −1.00 can reduce all risk

Often, clients ask me why one of their investments is not doing well when everything else is going up. My explanation typically revolves around correlation. If you are properly diversified, some of your investments will be decreasing in value as others are increasing. If you think about it, you don't want all of your investments to go up at the same time because, guess what happens when things start to go bad? . . . They will all go down at the same time.

If you take this concept one step forward, as it relates to your investment portfolio, your goal for diversification is to have non-correlating assets in your portfolio. However, that is easier said than done.

During the past 10 years, correlations, in general, have been increasing, making it difficult to diversify. For example, take a look at Figure 7.5 that shows the correlation of various asset classes in 2002 versus 2012.

Ten years ago, in 2002, it was almost twice as easy as it is today to diversify. In 2002, ten major asset classes provided moderate to substantial diversification to the S&P 500:

- Hedge Funds
- Commodities

2012 vs. 2002

Historical 5-Year Correlations of
Selected Asset Classes to the S&P 500

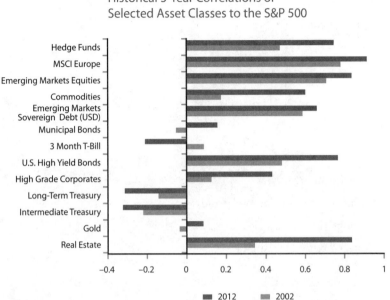

Figure 7.5: 2002 vs. 2012—The Correlation of Different Asset Classes
Source: Commonwealth Financial Network.
All indices are unmanaged and investors cannot actually invest directly into an index.
Unlike investments, indices do not incur management fees, charges, or expenses. Past
performance does not guarantee future results. Hedge Funds, Dow Jones Credit Suisse
Hedge Fund Index USD; MSCI Europe, MSCI Europe Index ND USD; Emerging Market
Equities, MSCI EM (Emerging Markets) Index ND USD; Commodities, Dow Jones-UBS
US Commodity Index TR; Emerging Markets Sovereign Debt (USD), JPM EMBI Global
Diversified Index TR USD; Municipal Bonds, Barclays Municipal Bond Index; 3-month
T-Bill, Bank of America Merrill Lynch 3-month U.S. Treasury Bill Index; U.S. High-Yield
Bonds, Bank of America U.S. High-Yield Master II Index TR USD; High-Grade
Corporates, Barclays U.S. Corp Investment-Grade Index TR USD; Long-Term Treasury,
Barclays Long-Term U.S. Treasury Index TR USD; Intermediate Treasury, Barclays
Intermediate Treasury Index TR USD; Gold, London Fix Gold PM PR USD; Real Estate,
Dow Jones U.S. Real Estate Index TR USD.

- Municipal Bonds
- 3-Month Treasuries
- U.S. High-Yield Bonds

- High-Grade Corporate Bonds
- Long-Term Treasuries
- Intermediate Treasuries
- Gold
- Real Estate

However, in 2012, that list dwindled down to only six main asset classes:

- Municipal Bonds
- 3-Month Treasuries
- High-Grade Corporate Bonds
- Long-Term Treasuries
- Intermediate Treasuries
- Gold

It should be noted that even though these asset classes do not exhaust the entire investment world, they do capture the greater part of what most investors use within their portfolios.

Bottom line: More investments are moving in tandem with the S&P 500, which makes diversifying more difficult.

2. Volatility Is Increasing

If you have been investing in equities for a long time, you can appreciate the fact that the S&P 500 Index has become more volatile. In fact, if you look back starting from the 1950s, an interesting picture (Figure 7.6) emerges:

As you see, the past decade was more volatile than the preceding 50 years *combined*! After creating this chart for the last decade and seeing the stark increase, I decided it would be worthwhile to look at the beginning of this decade to see if a trend was developing. My hunch was correct, for the period of January 1, 2010, through July 19, 2012, we had 20 days that the S&P 500 Index either increased or decreased

Number of Days with Moves Greater than ±3%

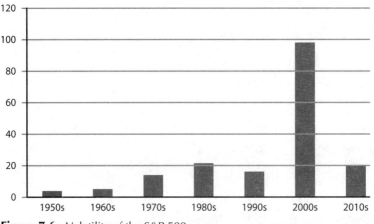

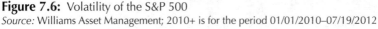

Figure 7.6: Volatility of the S&P 500
Source: Williams Asset Management; 2010+ is for the period 01/01/2010–07/19/2012

by 3 percent or more! In fact, the past couple of years has produced more moves of plus or minus 3 percent than the *entire 1990s!* If you extrapolate from this trend and believe it will continue, you will need to strap on your seat belts for a bumpy ride unless, of course, we can determine the right mixture of investments to help alleviate some of this volatility.

Let's take a look at some of the crisis events since 1970. But first, let me note that after World War II, market volatility dramatically declined and stayed stable for decades. We experienced increased volatility after market drops, for example, in 1973–1974 during the Oil Embargo. Then at the turn of the century, we had the tech bubble collapse (Tech Wreck) and 9/11, which led to a burst of volatility. It then diminished until the big increase in volatility came with our most recent financial crisis. The S&P 500 Index lost 57 percent from peak to trough during this crisis! Then the markets came back more than 100 percent (which is still a loss of 14%). Sometimes we forget the bad times too easily and often need reminders of why we are diversified, especially after run-ups in the market when it is easy to be overconfident. Here are some examples of the most significant financial crises during the past four decades:

- Oil Embargo: 1973–1974
- Secondary Banking Crisis: 1973–1975
- Latin American Debt Crisis: 1982
- Israel Bank Stock Crisis: 1983
- Black Monday: 1987
- S&L Crisis: 1989–1991
- Black Wednesday: 1992
- Mexican Peso Crisis: 1994
- Asian Financial Crisis: 1997
- Russian Financial Crisis: 1998
- Tech Wreck: 2000–2002
- Credit Crisis: 2007–2009
- Flash Crash: 2010
- PIIGS: 2010– (five Eurozone nations)
- Next Crisis???

Another factor in the increase in volatility is high-frequency trading. According to the *Wall Street Journal*, high-speed trading accounts for *more the half of the volume* of the stock market! This volume is up from 26 percent in 2006, according to market research[41] by the TABB Group.

With the help of powerful computers and algorithms, traders can place millions of orders a second and alter the order in milliseconds. These traders typically make a fraction of a cent at a time,

---

[41] *http://online.wsj.com/article/SB100014240527023036304045773922239535512 32.html*

multiplied by hundreds of shares, tens of thousands of times a day. High-frequency traders rarely, if ever, hold onto positions overnight. Algorithmic and high-frequency trading were both found to have contributed to volatility in the May 6, 2010, Flash Crash, when high-frequency liquidity providers were in fact found to have withdrawn from the market. The Dow plunged nearly 1,000 points during the Flash Crash only to rebound within minutes.

Ironically, as investors focus more on risk management, more volatility may occur—more selling when markets are falling and more buying when markets are increasing. This increased volume will further exacerbate price movements.

So, why does increased volatility of the stock market suggest that we need a different way to diversify? Volatility by itself doesn't suggest that we need a different way to diversify. However, when increased volatility is considered, coupled with the other five reasons we are discussing on this list, we become aware of the need to consider a change to our methodology.

3. Interest Rates Are Low

As I write this book in 2013, interest rates in the United States are at, or near, all-time lows. In fact, they have been on a fairly steady declining track for 30 years (see Figure 7.7)! Remember, you may be reading this book years after its publication; the interest rate environment is sure to have changed by then. However, I think this theme will last a long time, especially if we continue to see growth in the economy— another 30-year secular decline in interest rates is unlikely. With that said, if I am correct, some bonds, specifically ones that were the great diversifiers of the past decade (i.e., long-term Treasury and corporate bonds) may not perform as well in the future. While bonds may still help you diversify your portfolio, it will become more important to pay close attention to interest rate risk.

When (not if) interest rates increase, existing bonds will decrease in value. For example, let's suppose you bought a 10-year bond from Company A for $1,000 and it was paying 5 percent. Every year, you

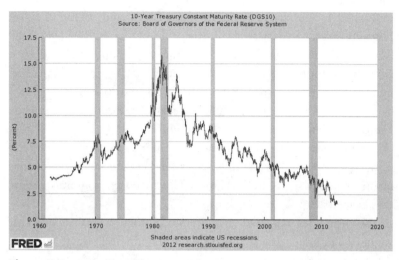

Figure 7.7: Treasury Yields at 30-Year Lows

would receive $50 in interest, and when the bond matures in 10 years, you would receive back your $1,000. One year from now, a new bond is issued by the same Company A, and it is paying 6 percent. If an investor had a choice to purchase your bond for $1,000 paying 5 percent or a new bond for $1,000 paying 6 percent, that investor would purchase the new bond. However, if the price of your bond decreased to $931 (and the investor would receive $1,000 at maturity), the decision is not as easy. In fact, the yield-to-maturity on these two bonds would be identical.

Now, if you own individual bonds (not bond mutual funds),[42] and you hold your bond to maturity, then you would receive back par, typically $1,000, for the bond. You still would have seen the value fluctuate over your holding period, but in the end you would not have lost money (assuming the company does not default or the bond was

---

[42]The purchase of bonds is subject to availability and market conditions. The relationship between the price of bonds and the yield is inverse: when price goes up, yield goes down, and vice versa. Market risk is a consideration if sold or redeemed prior to maturity. Some bonds have call features that may affect income. See the glossary for more detailed information on different types of bonds.

not called) if you held it to maturity. On the other hand, if you are like many bond investors who use mutual funds, you do not have the benefit of deciding whether to hold the bond to maturity; the fund manager(s) will make this decision. Therefore, you have the potential to lose money if interest rates increase and you are holding interest-rate-sensitive bonds.

So, if you agree that interest rates are at historical lows and have a high probability of increasing in the future, bonds may not be as good of a diversifier as in the past. Like correlations increasing, this probability is a reason for considering alternative ways to diversify.

4. Scammers, Scandals, and Mistrust

Greed and dishonesty have been around for our entire civilized life. You would think that after criminal minds see the fines, prison sentences, and embarrassment associated with the consequences of getting caught in a scandal, the criminal activity would stop or slow down substantially. Unfortunately, plenty of people may or may not be thinking of the consequences and are willing to cross moral, ethical, and legal boundaries to make more money.

Scammers are smart. Bernie Madoff didn't con people for more than 30 years and steal $65 billion dollars (according to federal regulators) from many sophisticated investors by being dumb. In another recent and brazen example, Robert Allen Stanford stole $7 billion dollars starting in 2006 by having believable marketing materials, slick sales people, and questionable philanthropic activities. Unfortunately, these examples are just two out of hundreds.

At what point does the average investor totally give up hope, throw up his or her arms in disgust? Does the Occupy Wall Street movement from 2011 grow and become stronger or does it fade away? This mistrust has been building for a long time and will take time, tougher laws, better oversight, and fewer (ideally none, but that is wishful thinking) scandals.

In the meantime, investors will need a more thorough due diligence process to minimize the risk of fraud. As investors' assets grow, diversifying among multiple asset managers and platforms may become more common as well.

5. Government/Sovereign Involvement

The governments and central banks of the world have a lot of power. Through fiscal policy, they can use taxation and expenditures to influence the economy. With monetary policy, governments, central banks, and monetary authorities can control the supply of money to promote economic growth and stability. We obviously need to have faith that these entities make good decisions.

The problem occurs when bad (or no) decisions are made.

Markets hate political uncertainty. In 2011, many Americans were appalled when partisan bickering between opposition Republicans and Democrats pushed the nation to the brink of default on its massive debts. The political gridlock is what prompted the downgrade of the U.S. credit rating. The debt ceiling deal that brought months of political squabbling to an end in 2011, culminated in the Budget Control Act, signed into law on August 2, 2011. A month earlier, on July 22, 2011, when the Democratic Senate voted to table the Cut, Cap, and Balance Act passed by the Republican House, the S&P 500 hit 1,345 points. Less than three weeks later, on August 8, the stock index had collapsed 16.8 percent to 1119 points, as markets bottomed out in the aftermath of the fateful credit downgrade.

In the 2012 election year, Congress had another debt-ceiling debate and fiscal cliff looming, with finger pointing more prevalent than problem solving. It is unfortunate that the inability of our representatives in government to work together and make bipartisan decisions can wreak havoc on our investments by driving stocks down. In August 2011, President Obama was addressing the nation as the world's stock exchanges plummeted in response to the indecision about raising the debt ceiling. President Obama stated that no matter what some agency (S&P) may say, the United States always has been and always will be a triple-A country. That was a few days after Standard & Poor's stripped us of our rating. Even while the president was speaking, the Dow fell below 11,000 for the first time in nine months.

So, even if the economy is doing well and you have created a well-diversified portfolio, all your efforts could be for naught if the government makes poor (or no) decisions—another reason we need to consider alternative strategies for diversification.

6. Deleveraging

Individuals and governments have built an enormous amount of debt. In 2000, global public debt was $19.1 trillion (59% of global GDP). In 2012, that number ballooned to $44.3 trillion (79% of global GDP)![43] This jump is not something that has gone unnoticed. Unfortunately, I do not believe (at least in the United States) we can fully grasp the long-term effect it will have on our economy.

How did we get here? The answer is not simple. It was a combination of three factors: human decisions, economic circumstance, and the cumulative effect of time. Back in 2001, the Congressional Budget Office (CBO) forecasted that in the next decade good things were to come, that between 2001 and 2011 the United States would run budget surpluses totaling $5.6 trillion. Unfortunately, the CBO does not have the ability to predict the future. They did not accurately foresee the "Great Recession" and the economic problems of the coming years. Nor did the CBO have the ability to know that Presidents Bush and Obama (first term) would reduce taxes to the extent they did. Lastly, discretionary spending increased substantially, including defense spending (due to the wars in Iraq and Afghanistan), homeland security upgrades, food stamps, and other safety-net programs. Bottom line, Uncle Sam spent more than he took in.

At some point in our future, we will need to "pay the piper." We will do so through deleveraging.

Without getting ahead of myself, and before I explain *de*leveraging and its impact to the economy, I want to explain leverage. Leverage, in the context of this section, means to use debt to increase your ability to purchase a much larger investment or item. Think about your home: you put down 20 percent as a down payment and the rest of the cost typically comes in the form of a mortgage from a bank. The bank's money allows you to "leverage" your money and purchase the home.

---

[43] *The Economist*, World Bank.

Too much debt ultimately leads to deleveraging. Think about deleveraging as the opposite of leverage; you reduce the amount of debt. More technically, according to McKinsey & Company, it is defined as an episode in which the ratio of total debt to GDP declines for at least three straight years and falls by 10 percent or more, or an episode in which the total stock of nominal credit in the economy declines by 10 percent or more. The four main parts of the economy that use leverage are households, corporations, commercial real estate, and governments.

Although not always, deleveraging typically follows a major financial crisis. And according to the McKinsey Global Institute, it lasts for six to seven years on average and reduces gross domestic product (GDP) by 25 percent.[44] The deleveraging process, therefore, exerts a significant drag on the growth of an economy.

As of this writing, only a small amount of deleveraging occurred since the "Great Recession," due primarily to the fact that increases in government debt offset the declines in household debt and commercial real estate. The massive amount of government debt throughout the world economies could likely result in years of austerity ("belt tightening"), and possible defaults and high inflation. Most likely, austerity will play the biggest role in deleveraging, as we have already started to see in Europe. We face a real risk of a fragile and prolonged unstable global economy with slow GDP growth. If this slow-growth scenario comes to fruition, as I believe it will, stock markets may face substantial headwinds.

For this explicit reason, we may need to change the methods of our diversification strategies. In other words, slow growth, due to deleveraging, may cause stocks not to perform to our growth expectations, and we could need to potentially find alternatives to stocks for investment returns.

---

[44] McKinsey & Company, "Debt and deleveraging: The global credit bubble and its economic consequences," January 2010.

Over time, some of these six reasons will change, but the point to consider is that we need to adapt to both long-term trends as well as shorter-term economic factors.

INVESTORS (AND ADVISORS) ARE QUESTIONING THE OLD RULES

The market decline, from October 2007 to early March 2009, was the worst since the late 1930s. Stocks dropped 60 percent, investor uncertainty skyrocketed, and trust and confidence were shattered. Financial advisors and their clients questioned the age-old rules for investing: Is buy-and-hold dead? Has asset allocation outlived its usefulness? Does diversification still work? Everything we have been discussing in this chapter has led to these questions. As mentioned earlier, the message is that we need to be aware that times change, and with changing times comes the need to be flexible and to have the ability to change diversification strategies.

Because no one knows what's going to happen in the market next, you need to treat asset allocation and security selection as equals in the portfolio-building process. You need to determine how much risk you're willing to take on and what your goals are. Then you (or you and your financial advisor) can build your asset mix around them and try to maximize your return within each asset class by choosing great investments.[45]

Peter Kraus, the CEO and chair of asset management giant Alliance Bernstein, is quoted as saying during a meeting with stock analysts, "Put simply, the fundamental rules of prudent long-term investing aren't working." Investors should not be afraid to change their own rules of investing. Even legendary value investor Warren Buffett felt the need to tweak some of the lessons and strategies he learned from his mentors, Benjamin Graham and Philip Fisher. Two decades ago, Buffett wouldn't touch a technology stock with a ten-foot pole. Today he owns a massive amount of IBM and a hunk of Intel. The

---

[45]*http://news.morningstar.com/classroom2/printlesson.asp?docId=4506&CN*

point here is simple: Adapting your strategy to evolving markets is
sometimes necessary.

THE TIMES ARE A-CHANGIN' FOR ARTISTS AND FOR INVESTORS

For artists, making and mixing oil paint is a challenging, time-
consuming activity, and one can only imagine the difficulties Michelangelo faced when painting his huge, highly detailed works of
art. Mixing and maintaining both the consistency and color of his
paint while creating his Sistine Chapel masterpiece must have been
extremely difficult, and not unlike the challenges investors face when
trying to decide the proper mix and allocation of their investments.
Even though we know that Michelangelo's use of color on his masterpieces has lasted for centuries, his use of color was criticized by some
as being unsuitable. By considering the lighting conditions, both then
and now, it will help to explain Michelangelo's unexpected use of
vivid color at times. We could certainly draw a parallel to today's market conditions and the discussions/controversies about the various
strategies of asset allocation and diversification of current investment
portfolios. Yesterday's concepts (while time-honored) used in today's
economic and market conditions may not be suitable for investors.

In this chapter we presented the information we believe you need
to build a resilient portfolio with the expectation that it can survive
the market cycles that are an inevitable part of investing. We also explained the concept of diversification and asset allocation, as well as
past theories and strategies that have shaped current beliefs and investment philosophies. Perhaps we have relied too heavily on these strategies without being flexible enough to adapt to the changing world
economies. We may need to change the way we diversify our portfolios. We will learn what to do differently in the next chapter.

8 | Create the Masterpiece—A Resilient Investment Portfolio

> *"The marble not yet carved can hold the form of every thought the greatest artist has."*
>
> —Michelangelo

MICHELANGELO CREATED MANY MASTERPIECES DURING HIS LIFE. HE designed the iconic dome of St. Peter's Basilica in Rome (although its completion came after his death), *Moses* (a sculpture completed 1515); *The Last Judgment* (a painting completed 1534); and *Day, Night, Dawn*, and *Dusk* (sculptures, all completed by 1533). Each of these individually puts Michelangelo in the category of artistic genius, but taken together they undeniably make him a master of art for all ages.

In another artistic treasure, Michelangelo painted twelve figures—seven prophets and five sibyls (female prophets of myth)—around the border of the ceiling of the Sistine Chapel, and filled the central space with scenes from Genesis. The ceiling of the Sistine Chapel is a combination of individual works of art that separately could be considered treasures, but as a whole, make a masterpiece. Think about your life for a moment. It contains many different elements you may cherish or appreciate. What is on your list? I would venture to say, for many, the list would include career, marriage, children, friendships, philanthropy, and an enjoyable retirement. How does money fit into this list? It is the investment portfolio, most likely created by a successful career and a discipline of saving, that will allow you to achieve your goals in life.

Your investment portfolio is the centerpiece of your masterpiece and, like the twelve figures on the Sistine Chapel, a masterpiece within the masterpiece called "Life." If done properly and sufficiently, your investments have the potential to provide financial support to raise and educate your children. Your investment portfolio might allow you to support the causes and charities that are important to you. Ultimately, the goal of your investments is to allow you to live a fulfilling retirement and maybe pass along your wealth to future generations.

Keep in mind though, your investment portfolio is not a scorecard to keep track of how "rich" you are. Instead, it is limited resource that you will use to help you achieve the quality of life that you want for yourself and your family.

As you read this book, you are in the process of creating the masterpiece called "Life." Remember, life is a work in progress, and your investment portfolio is part of this progress. It is a masterpiece, much like Michelangelo's design of the dome of St. Peter's, that will continue to be valued beyond your life.

WHAT HAVE WE LEARNED SO FAR?

After having read Chapters 6 and 7, it is my hope that you have come to conclusions similar to the following:

- It is difficult, if not impossible, to successfully time the market consistently.

- It is becoming more difficult to diversify portfolios due to the high correlation of traditional investments.

- Determining your risk tolerance is the most important (and first) step to building a resilient portfolio.

- Bonds, especially if interest rates rise, may not be as good of a diversifier as they have been in the past.

- The stock market has become more volatile in the last decade and this trend (based on this decade so far) may continue.

- Many of the traditional investment classes (U.S. bonds and stocks) have become more efficient and, therefore, less likely to beat their respective index. We will discuss this topic in greater detail later in the chapter.

- High-frequency trading characterizes the majority of stock transactions and puts the individual investor at a disadvantage.

- We may be in a long-term cycle of slow growth due to deleveraging and other factors that could adversely affect stock market performance.

Let's use what we have learned so far and build a *resilient portfolio*.

A RESILIENT PORTFOLIO

In this section, we will build on what you have previously learned: After determining your risk tolerance, diversification is the most important part of building an investment portfolio because it can help you potentially increase returns while minimizing risk (and sometimes the anxiety that comes with investing in equities).

Because of the number of securities and investments available, the infinite combination of possible allocations, and your unique time frame, risk tolerance, and tax considerations, trying to provide *you* specific advice could make this a lengthy book. Therefore, we will draw a blueprint and build a foundation: a solid understanding of some common (and uncommon) concepts and strategies that can educate you about investment planning. Implementation or building of your investment portfolio will be done by either your financial advisor or you, depending on your preference. Later in the book, we will discuss how to make that decision.

One last point I want to make before we start the process of building a resilient portfolio: *You need to have a long-term time horizon to invest.* Many investment industry professionals would have you think three to five years is considered long term. However, I think we need a new mentality and to think in terms of five to ten or more years. This suggestion applies even if you are 60 or 70 years old, because you could very well live into your eighties or nineties.

Key Point: *Investing requires patience.*

Now, if you are on board, let's talk about building a resilient portfolio!

THE FIVE STEPS TO BUILDING A RESILIENT PORTFOLIO

Step 1: Determine your risk level.

Step 2: Determine your asset allocation.

Step 3: Select your investments.

Step 4: Monitor your investments.

Step 5: Document your process.

Step 1: Determine Your Overall Risk Level.

In Chapter 6, we explained how to assess whether you are a conservative, moderately conservative, moderate, moderately aggressive, or aggressive investor. We also learned that some accounts may be more aggressive than others. For example, if you are drawing income, or expect to draw from your portfolio within one to three years, that particular account (that you plan to draw income from) should be no more risky than "moderate" and *preferably* moderately conservative or conservative, depending on your specific feelings about risk. We want to attempt to *minimize the volatility in this part of your portfolio.*

Conversely, some of your accounts may be invested more aggressively. For example, as I mentioned in Chapter 6, if you determine that you have an account that stands a good chance of not being used in your lifetime, you may want to consider investing that account more

aggressively. The most important point is
that your overall portfolio should match
your risk tolerance.

Step 2: Determine Your Asset Allocation.

The goal of asset allocation is to optimize a
portfolio. In other words, the goal is to determine the mix of investments that, when
combined together in a specific way, will attempt to minimize risk and maximize return.

Most professional investors and institutions would agree that asset allocation (i.e.,

> **Key Point:** *Your
> overall portfolio
> should match your
> risk tolerance. Some
> accounts may be
> more aggressive
> and some may be
> more conservative,
> depending on your
> time frame and needs.*

how much goes into stocks, bonds, etc.) is an important factor in the
building of your investment portfolio, but some noisemakers would have
you think differently. Some so-called experts would have you believe
that asset allocation is "dead" because many traditional portfolios performed poorly in crisis situations. (Remember the 60/40 portfolio from
Chapter 7 lost 30%+ in the downturn of 2007–2009.) Don't believe
this "noise." Diversification, through the use of asset allocation, is a vital
factor in building your portfolio. However, the reason may not be what
you think it is. It is not because of some complicated formula that only
a mathematician would understand. Nor is it because of the laws of
finance. It is because of the behavioral result of how we manage our
investments.

You see, if humans did not have emotions and a short-term memory
(and financial advisors and endowment managers did not have clients who
could fire them), everyone would just invest in small-cap stocks and "call
it a day." The reason is small-cap stocks have had the best returns when
compared to large-cap stocks, bonds, and cash (as well as other traditional
investments) over a long period of time; from 1926 to 2011, small-cap
stocks averaged 11.88 percent.[46] However, investors, including individuals,
institutions, and endowments, do not have the patience to withstand the
pain of a downturn. For example, small-cap stocks, as measured by the

---

[46] John Hancock, "A Special Focus on Volatility and the Financial Markets," p. 1.

Russell 2000 Index, lost 21.46 percent in 1990, 21.58 percent in 2002, and 34.80 percent in 2008. It is difficult to watch your portfolio fall by 20 to 35 percent! It becomes even more painful if you are withdrawing from your retirement accounts while their value is dropping (and as mentioned previously, that is why you should consider withdrawing from a portfolio that is conservative or moderately conservative during retirement). A financial advisor or endowment manager who only bought and held small-cap stocks for your entire portfolio would lose his or her job. Even though it might have been the best place to invest over the long term, investors just don't have enough patience.

To alleviate the emotional pain of losing money during downturns and to avoid the risk of swinging the pendulum of selling "everything" in moments of crisis, professional investors, as well as individuals, have agreed that asset allocation is the way to go. Asset allocation does not protect your portfolio against a loss in declining markets, but

> **Key Point:** *Most investors can't stomach the emotional pain of extreme volatility, and asset allocation can potentially help minimize both.*

it may reduce volatility. No program can guarantee that any objective or goal will be achieved.

So, how do you create an asset allocation model that is appropriate for your risk tolerance? You have two options:

Option 1: You can rely on your financial advisor's guidance and expertise. We will talk more about how to find a competent advisor in Chapter 10.

Option 2: You can rely on a model provided by a mutual fund company, based on your risk tolerance. Many large mutual fund institutions provide model portfolios, as well as basic asset allocation calculators, based on different risk classifications. Alternatively, you can purchase software to help you determine your asset allocation model; many choices are available, ranging in price from free to thousands of dollars. Using software provided through mutual fund websites is typically free but does have its drawbacks. The main drawback being that it may limit you to the types of investments the program considers. For example, it may only consider mutual funds or exchange-traded products. Or the model may be too general; while it may call for U.S. stocks, it may not specifically show how much should be allocated to large vs. small caps. Lastly, it might not include alternative investments in its models. I will discuss alternative investments a little later in this chapter.

The one caveat when it comes to software is the human factor. Because you or your advisor may have the ability to constrain the model (i.e., reduce the percentage allocated to stocks), this action can essentially invalidate the optimized portfolio. Although taking such an action is not necessarily a bad thing because some software tools will suggest that you have a substantial portion in aggressive investments, such as small-cap stocks, it may not be appropriate for your situation. Your knowledge of investments will come into play here, which is where *art* and science collide.

Word of caution: Unfortunately, many investors—both individuals and institutions alike—chase performance. Investors become impatient with investments that are not doing well and want to move those funds to investments that *have* done well. The common result, especially for individuals, is that they buy too late, at or near the top, and then they sell too late, at or near the bottom. They get beat up on both sides (See Figure 6.6). Now, with that being said, in a couple of instances an investor *might want to* consider the following two strategies.

One important move would be when you rebalance your portfolio. The act of rebalancing forces you to sell the *relatively* better-performing investments and buy the *relatively* poorer-performing investments. Buy low. Sell high. That's the name of the game. It is simply the process of restoring your portfolio back to the original allocation you had selected. For example, and to keep it simple, let's suppose you determine that you should have a portfolio of 25 percent stocks, 25 percent bonds, 25 percent cash, and 25 percent real estate. Over time, let's suppose stocks performed far better than the other asset classes and now represent 40 percent of your portfolio. Knowing that 40 percent in stocks is more risk than you want to take on, you would simply restore your stock allocation back down to the original 25 percent allocation. Taking the example one step further, assume that the bond allocation has decreased from 25 percent to 15 percent of the portfolio. After you sell 15 percent of your stock allocation, you would increase your bond allocation by 10 percent. This rebalancing is the "science" part of investment management, the *paint-by-number* part of investing—it's easy to do.

Figure 8.1 shows us that while a portfolio of 60 percent stocks and 40 percent bonds, as represented by the indices mentioned, might have performed well over this time frame; you may have reduced your risk by 17 percent *and* increased your returns slightly by rebalancing.

So, how often should you rebalance? The answer to this question is up for debate. Some of the most commonly used strategies include the following:

- **Time period.** Most common is semi-annually or annually. You simply rebalance on this frequency, regardless of the percentage change. For example, on January 15 of every year, you rebalance.

The Benefits of Rebalancing

30 Year Monthly Rebalancing: 10/1/1982–8/31/2012

Initial Portfolio — Barclays U.S. Aggregate Index / S&P 500 Index — 60% / 40%

Buy and Hold — Barclays U.S. Aggregate Index 23% / S&P 500 Index 77%
Return: 10.45%
St Dev: 11.85%

Rebalanced — Barclays U.S. Aggregate Index 40% / S&P 500 Index 60%
Return: 10.50%
St Dev: 9.80%

•Monthly Rebalancing creates a higher return figure while also reducing risk within the portfolio by not allowing the portfolio to stray from its target allocation

Figure 8.1: The Benefits of Rebalancing
Source: Commonwealth Financial Network.
Initial hypothetical portfolios comprised of 60% S&P 500, 40% Barclays Capital U.S. Aggregate Bonds. Risk equals historical annualized standard deviation. For illustration only. Past performance is not a guarantee of future results. Investors cannot invest directly in an index. Portfolio re-balancing may include trading costs and fees.

- **5% rule.** Simply rebalance the portfolio if the target allocation deviates more than 5 percent. For example, if you have a target of 5 percent allocated to large-cap stocks and large-cap stocks are now 11 percent, then you sell the excess 6 percent and move those proceeds to the asset class(es) that are below their target.

- **Combination approach.** This method suggests that you rebalance based on the time period but only if the deviation (call this your trigger event) exceeds the target allocation by 5 percent.

- **Variance from the target.** This method involves looking at how far the asset class has drifted away from the target while considering other asset classes in your model. For example, you determine that you want to rebalance if the target deviates by 25 percent. As an illustration, if you have a target for high-grade corporate bonds of 40 percent, you would rebalance if high-grade bonds decreased below 30 percent or above 50 percent (i.e., 40% × 0.75 or 40% × 1.25). You could also use a time period with this strategy (similar to the combination approach).

Which method you choose is less important than having a process that is consistent.

Rebalancing may also involve a few drawbacks. They include:

- Transaction costs—buying and selling certain investments may have costs.

- Taxes—in a nonqualified account (i.e., taxable), when you sell an investment that has an unrealized (appreciation) gain, you may have to pay capital gains taxes.

Even with the potential drawbacks, rebalancing can be a simple way to attempt to ensure your portfolio doesn't become more risky than intended over time.

> **Key Point:** *Faithfully adhering to rebalancing through a documented process may help you make sure your portfolio doesn't become more risky over time and might improve your returns.*

The second move that deserves potential consideration is buying and selling based on fundamental or technical analysis. For example, if a class of stocks looks expensive relative to historical data, you might reduce the percentage allocated to that particular asset class. Some of the key fundamentals you might consider reviewing regularly would be price-to-earnings, price-to-sales, and price-to-cash flow ratios from the past five years, relative to today's statistics. However, the great thing about a *well-diversified* portfolio is that you don't have to worry as much about valuations or technical analysis. Again, here is where science and art intersect.

Note that I did not say you should sell an entire asset class if it looks expensive or because some "expert" on television says to. Although you may take this action due to changes in your asset allocation (i.e., you change your risk tolerance or the risk/return/correlation of an investment class no longer fits into the model), selling an entire asset class due to market concerns is typically unwarranted. You don't have to swing the pendulum from one extreme to another.

Savvy investors are saying to themselves right now, "Gary, tell me something I don't know." You see, what I have discussed is widely agreed to and accepted. Although Warren Buffett may disagree with what I have said, for most mortals it is the typical basis for building a portfolio.

Let's move on to where you will begin to appreciate (if you haven't already) the idea of an *art* to investment management, or selecting your investments.

Step 3: Select Your Investment.

In this step, we will take the knowledge you have gained thus far and determine which investments will best "fill" your model.

The four main types of investments for your consideration include the following:[47]

---

[47] Please remember that all investments are subject to risk, including the loss of principal. Because investment return and principal value fluctuate, shares may be worth more or less than their original value. Some investments are not suitable for all investors, and there is no guarantee that any investing goal will be met. **Past performance is no guarantee of future results. Please consider the investment objectives, risks, charges, and expenses carefully before investing. The prospectus, which contains this and other**

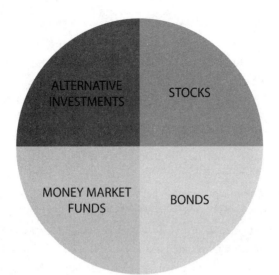

- Stocks
- Bonds
- Money Market Funds
- Alternatives

Each of these asset classes includes many different investment options and products to consider. It reminds me of when I was young and having fun with coloring books. I remember using a box of 64 Crayola Crayons and thinking there were too many choices. Really, who needed Piggy Pink, Pink Flamingo, Pink Sherbet, Tickle Me Pink, and Carnation Pink? One pink was more than enough for me! In the investment world, we have lots of choices, too, and it can be overwhelming. For example, mutual funds have grown in number from 1,243 in 1984 to 7,637 in 2011.[48] Exchange-traded funds, another popular investment vehicle, have grown in number from 1 in 1993 to 1,134

---

information about the investment, can be obtained from your financial professional. Be sure to read the prospectus carefully before deciding whether to invest.

[48] 2012 Investment Company Fact Book, p. 138.

in 2011![49] They are just two types of investment products. When you consider others, such as separately managed accounts, closed-end funds, stocks, bonds, hedge funds, and so on, you can quickly see that your choices are substantial (and growing rapidly).

Although I wish I could teach you both the science and the *art* of investment selection in this chapter, no magic pill will turn you into a Warren Buffett. In other words, the process of investment selection alone could turn into a lengthy thesis. My hope is that once you finish reading this material, you will have an appreciation of the selection *process*. I hope you become educated (and more open-minded, if you aren't already) to potential investments for your portfolio that may help you lower the correlation between your investments (i.e., diversify), as well as potentially reduce your risk and increase your returns. Ultimately, if you are working with a financial advisor, you can rely on his or her expertise. However, if you are working without the help of a professional advisor, then you will need to become well-educated in how to select your investment strategy and/or manager.

STOCKS AND BONDS

Trying to select stock and bond investments that regularly beat a particular market consistently is difficult on a risk-adjusted basis (i.e., a higher return with the same amount of risk). Throw in transaction costs, which could include trading costs or the cost of fund companies hiring consultants and analysts, and it becomes difficult to beat the markets.

A tremendous amount of research has led to these conclusions. Of the many notable economists who have studied this subject, dating back to the 1900s, two stand out in my mind. The first, Harry Markowitz, also known as the "father of portfolio management," was briefly mentioned in the previous chapter. In the 1950s, he created the "efficient frontier," which determined an "optimal" portfolio (a portfolio that maximized return for a given level of risk). His Nobel Prize–winning approach, called modern portfolio theory, is also referred to as MPT. The second economist who stands out for me is Eugene Fama. In the 1960s, he developed the efficient market hypothesis (EMH)

---

[49] 2012 Investment Company Fact Book, p. 147.

at the University of Chicago Booth School of Business. EMH suggests that active managers cannot beat the markets on a risk-adjusted basis because it has already priced in all publicly known information.

In other research that supported Markowitz and Fama and according to Robert Arnott, financial analyst and author, Dr. Andrew Berkin, a PhD in structured investment management, and Jia Ye, investment researcher, using market returns over a 20-year period, found that the odds of an actively managed mutual fund beating the overall market index were just 5–22 percent before taxes and 4–14 percent after taxes, with average margins of defeat approximately twice as large as the average margins of victory.[50]

In addition to the efficiency of the market and transaction costs, another reason why security selection plays a minimal role is due to something called survivorship bias. Survivorship bias is when investment firms simply get rid of, by merging with another investment or closing the investment, the investment products that don't perform well. While not discussed often, this process "hides the data" that further conclude that active management has a tough time beating its respective benchmark.

When you consider the efficiencies of market and survivorship bias, it becomes clear that some markets are difficult to beat with active managers. According to "The Case for Indexing," a white paper from Vanguard, April 2012 (see Figure 8.2), that covered 15 years of data (as of December 31, 2011):

- Only 31 percent of active managers in the large-cap blend category beat its benchmark (S&P 500 Index). When you adjust for survivorship bias, that number becomes only 16 percent!

- Only 7 percent of active managers in the mid-cap blend category beat its benchmark (S&P 400 Index). When you adjust for survivorship bias, that number becomes only 4 percent!

- Only 9 percent of active managers in the small-cap blend category beat its benchmark (S&P 600 Index). When you adjust for survivorship bias, that number becomes only 5 percent!

---

[50] See David Swensen, *Unconventional Success: A Fundamental Approach to Personal Investment* (New York: Free Press, 2005), pp. 213–217.

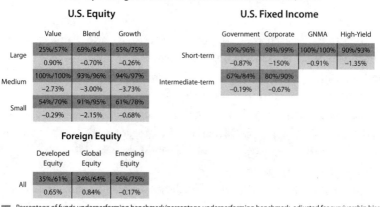

Relative Performance of U.S.-Domiciled
Actively Managed Funds: 15 Years as of December 31, 2011

U.S. Equity

	Value	Blend	Growth
Large	25%/57%	69%/84%	55%/75%
	0.90%	−0.70%	−0.26%
Medium	100%/100%	93%/96%	94%/97%
	−2.73%	−3.00%	−3.73%
Small	54%/70%	91%/95%	61%/78%
	−0.29%	−2.15%	−0.68%

U.S. Fixed Income

	Government	Corporate	GNMA	High-Yield
Short-term	89%/96%	98%/99%	100%/100%	90%/93%
	−0.87%	−150%	−0.91%	−1.35%
Intermediate-term	67%/84%	80%/90%		
	−0.19%	−0.67%		

Foreign Equity

	Developed Equity	Global Equity	Emerging Equity
All	35%/61%	34%/64%	56%/75%
	0.65%	0.84%	−0.17%

▬ Percentage of funds underperforming benchmark/percentage underperforming benchmark, adjusted for survivorship bias
▨ Median surviving fund excess return versus benchmark

Note: Performance data reflect 15 years through December 31, 2011.

Figure 8.2: Active Managers vs. Indexes
Source: ©Vanguard Group, Inc., used with permission.
Vanguard calculations, using data from Morningstar, Inc., MSCI, Standard & Poor's, and
Barclay Capital. Equity benchmarks represented by the following indexes: Large blend—
Standard & Poor's 500 Index, 1/1997 through 11/2002, and MSCI U.S. Prime Market 750
Index thereafter; Large value—S&P 500 Value Index, 1/1997 through 11/2002, and MSCI
U.S. Prime Market 750 Value Index thereafter; Large growth—S&P 500 Growth Index,
1/1997 through 11/2002, and MSCI U.S. Prime Market 750 GrowthIndex thereafter;
Medium blend—S&P MidCap 400 Index, 1/1997 through 11/2002, and MSCI U.S. MidCap
450 Index thereafter; Medium value—S&P MidCap 400 Value Index, 1/1997 through
11/2002, and MSCI U.S. Mid Cap 450 Value thereafter; Medium growth—S&P MidCap
400 Growth Index, 1/1997 through 11/2002, and MSCI U.S. Mid Cap 450 Growth Index
thereafter; Small blend—S&P SmallCap 600 Index, 1/1997 through 11/2002, and MSCI
U.S. Small Cap 1750 Index thereafter; Small value—S&P SmallCap 600 Value Index,
1/1997 through 11/2002, and MSCI U.S. Small Cap 1750 Value Index thereafter; Small
growth—S&P SmallCap 600 Growth Index, 1/1997 through 11/2002, and MSCI U.S. Small
Cap 1750 Growth Index thereafter. Bond benchmarks represented by the following Barclays
Capital indexes: U.S. 1–5 Year Government Bond Index, U.S. 1–5 Year Credit Bond Index,
U.S. Intermediate Government Bond Index, U.S. Intermediate Credit Bond Index, U.S.
GNMA Bond Index, U.S. Corporate High Yield Bond Index. International and global
benchmarks include the following MSCI indexes: EAFE Index, All Country World Index,
and Emerging Markets Index.

One asset class that doesn't appear to be as efficient as U.S. stock
funds is foreign equity. According to the same report from Vanguard:

- 65 percent of actively managed developed foreign equity (as
  compared to EAFE Index) funds, 66 percent of actively managed

global equity (as compared to the All Country World Index), and 44 percent of actively managed emerging equity funds (as compared to Emerging Markets Index) beat their benchmarks during that same period. The numbers decrease to 39 percent, 36 percent, and 25 percent, respectively, when considering survivorship bias.

Even though bond markets also appear to be efficient, active management in the future may add value. Remember our discussion on interest rates in Chapter7? Because interest rates are at or near all-time lows, bond prices may be adversely affected when interest rates ultimately rise. Active management may be able to navigate potential headwinds by managing this risk prudently.

Want more proof? As you can see in Figure 8.3, the difference between the top and bottom managers' performance in traditional investments (U.S. fixed income- and equity-based) is small. For example, only 1.2 percent separated the best from the worst U.S. large cap managers! Think about that for a moment. It is indicative of the efficiency of these markets, as mentioned previously.

Performance Difference Between Top and Bottom Quartile Managers 10 Years Ending September 2011

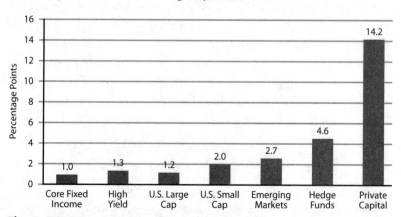

Figure 8.3: Asset Managers Are Bunched Together
Source: Lipper, a Thomson Reuters Company; Thomson Venture Economics; PerTrac; HFR (Hedge Fund Research, Inc.); Fund Evaluation Group, LLC

As the saying goes, "If you can't beat 'em, join 'em." For the asset classes that are efficient, one possible strategy is not to waste your energy or additional costs to try and beat the index. For example, if you determine in your asset allocation model that large-cap stocks are appropriate, you might consider investing in a mutual fund or exchange-traded fund that mimics the performance of a broad index that invests in large-cap stocks (i.e., S&P 500 Index).

> **Key Point:** *Using index-based investments may be an appropriate strategy for a significant part of your portfolio.*[51]

If you decide that you want to use actively managed investments, such as non-index-based mutual funds, that attempt to perform better than their respective index, how do you select the investments? Although performance is certainly a factor, it is not the only factor, and possibly not the most important one. Unfortunately, using historical performance is the most common way novice investors choose investments. I believe a better way is to consider risk-adjusted performance.[52] For example, if Investment A, a large-cap stock fund, has a five-year average return of 10 percent and Investment B, a similar investment, has a five-year average return of 9 percent, many would choose Investment A. However, if we determine through risk analysis, that Investment A takes five times as much risk as Investment B, do you think Investment A is still a better choice? Everything else being identical, I would select Investment B.

Although the risk of two investments or an actively managed investment and an index can be compared in a variety of ways, two of my favorites are Sharpe ratio and alpha. A detailed discussion on the Sharpe ratio and alpha are beyond the scope of this book, but I have

---

[51] In an actively managed fund, such as a mutual fund, the fund manager researches securities, and then buys and sells positions in an attempt to beat a particular market index. Passively managed funds, such as index funds or exchange-traded funds, typically invest in the same securities that make up a particular market index in an attempt to match the performance of the index. Because less work is involved with managing passive funds, they tend to have lower fees than actively managed funds.

[52] Risk-adjusted return: A measure of how much money your fund made relative to the amount of risk it took on over a specific time period.

included some material in the Disclosures and Definitions section if you are inclined to learn more.

You should also factor in the fees of the investments you are considering, because they can affect performance. Minimizing fees is straightforward and important. However, sometimes the process of focusing on investment costs consumes investors, and they may overlook otherwise good investments. Remember, some investments cost more than others, and fees, while extremely important to minimize, should not be the sole criteria used to select investments.

ALTERNATIVE INVESTMENTS[53]

What about asset classes that are less efficient, such as hedge funds and private equity? (See Figure 8.3.) These investments are referred to as alternative investments. The reason these investments are called "alternatives" is because they are, by definition, unconventional. That doesn't mean they are necessarily riskier than stocks but they can be. They may be different from the investments you have chosen in the past. That is okay. Becoming aware of alternative investments and why you might want to consider them in your portfolio will allow you to make an educated decision. Once you have familiarized yourself with them, they will be less "scary" and you may become more comfortable. Like everything in life, if you don't understand something, that doesn't mean it is a bad thing. It simply means that you have an opportunity to learn.

Many different investments are considered "alternatives." Some of the most widely used alternative investments include hedge funds and private investments, such as private equity, real estate, and energy/ natural resources.

According to the Securities and Exchange Commission, the definition of a hedge fund is:

> *Hedge funds pool money from investors and invest in securities or other types of investments with the goal of getting positive returns. Hedge*

---

[53] Investing in alternative investments may not be suitable for all investors and involves special risks, such as risk associated with leveraging the investment, potential adverse market forces, regulatory changes, and potential illiquidity. There is no assurance that the investment objective will be attained.

funds are not regulated as heavily as mutual funds and generally have more leeway than mutual funds to pursue investments and strategies that may increase the risk of investment losses. Hedge funds are limited to wealthier investors who can afford the higher fees and risks of hedge fund investing, and institutional investors, including some pension funds.[54]

Some examples of hedge funds include (a detailed description is found in the Disclosures and Definitions section in the back of this book):

- Opportunistic Equity: Long/Short Equity
- Enhanced Fixed Income: Long/Short Credit
- Absolute Return: Equity Market Neutral, Convertible Arbitrage, Fixed-Income Arbitrage, Event-Driven
- Tactical Trading: Commodities, Global Macro, Managed Futures

Private equity is a common term for investments that are typically made in nonpublic companies through privately negotiated transactions.[55] Private equity investments may be structured using a range of financial instruments, including common and preferred equity, convertible securities, subordinated debt, and warrants or other derivatives, depending on the strategy of the investor and the financing requirements of the company.[56] Types of private equity include:

---

[54] Hedge funds are not suitable for all investors, as they involve a high degree of risk and are speculative. The risks include, but are not limited to, the following: the funds may be leveraged; investors could lose all or a substantial amount of their investment; higher fees and expenses may be charged, which may increase the risk that returns are reduced; performance can be volatile; the funds are illiquid and there may be restrictions on transferring fund investments; there are other specific risks related to particular fund's investment strategies. Past performance does not guarantee future results. Investors must meet specific suitability standards before investing.

[55] Private equity investments have special and significant risks and are not suitable for all investors. The majority of private equity consists of institutional investors and accredited investors who can commit large sums of money for long periods of time.

[56] Partners Group.

- Buyout: Investments in established, cash-flow-positive companies. It is the most common type of private equity.
- Venture/growth: Investments in new and emerging companies. These investments typically are in companies with faster growth prospects than buyout companies with less use of leverage.
- Special situations: This broad category could include distressed companies, turnarounds, and mezzanine debt.

Other types of private investments may include real estate or energy and natural resources. Energy/natural resources investing includes the exploration, production, and transportation of gas, oil, and other fuel sources. This asset class could also include natural commodities like base metals (i.e., steel), precious metals (i.e., gold), or timber. Alternative energy and "green energy" could also be investments found in this category. Real estate could include commercial buildings, such as office complexes or apartment buildings, that typically include high levels of current cash flow. A more detailed description is beyond the scope of this book. Suffice it to say that entire books have been devoted to each of these categories.

Even though the types of investments I have mentioned are far from a complete list of alternatives, you can begin to appreciate the names of the different classes and the fact that many, if not all of these names, may be new to you. You may be saying, "Gary, this is complicated." Or you may be saying, "This is overwhelming." Well, if you are saying it, you are correct. It is complicated, and it can be overwhelming. Nobody said it would be easy, and I have devoted my entire career to studying this subject. Of course, trying to confuse you is not my intention. As I mentioned earlier in this book, I understand it is easy to become frustrated when learning something that is new, especially if you do not have interest in the subject matter. The reality of this subject matter is that it is complicated. However, what I can do is help educate you on some basic tenets of investment management so you can be well-informed and then can determine whether you want to educate yourself further. You have three choices at this point:

1. You can read the rest of this chapter and gain more knowledge. However, ultimately, if you want to implement a portfolio without the assistance of a financial advisor, understand that it will take time to become well-versed in financial topics, concepts, theories, and products, to name a few. I will be discussing this concept further in Chapter 9.

2. You can read on and become an educated investor who also relies on help from a professional. I will discuss how to select a financial advisor in Chapter 10.

3. Or you can throw up your arms and say, "I am going to sleep," setting this book down on your bedside table and counting sheep. I hope you don't select this option, but if you decide that this information is just too much to tackle, or you lack interest to do so, you can simply skip to Step 4 (see page 164).

If you choose Option 1 of the preceding choices, you will need to spend time with appropriate research. This time-consuming process includes a comprehensive identification, selection and qualification, and due diligence process supported by ongoing monitoring to ensure manager excellence.

If you choose Option 2, you don't necessarily need to know the ins and outs of each of these investment types or strategies your advisor employs. You should know, in general, why using alternative investments might be considered as a potential part of your investment implementation—by becoming an educated investor. Read on.

You may be saying, "Why not just keep it simple and use passive index investments or plain vanilla stock and bond mutual funds?" You definitely can! You just need to appreciate the fact that you may have the potential to do better with alternative investments, if they are right for you. Simply put, the possible benefits of some alternative investments include (a) increased diversification due to low correlations, and (b) historically lower volatility (see Figures 8.4 to 8.6). But it's important to remember the risks associated with alternatives, as mentioned previously, and that past volatility is not a guarantee of future and similar volatility.

To illustrate this point, we will compare various hedge fund strategies.

As you may remember from Chapter 7, investments that have lower correlations can provide you with increased diversification. Our goal is to find investments that are noncorrelated to one another. More specifically, to find investments that have a correlation between −.5 and +.5.

To understand the following table (Figure 8.4), look at the type of investment in the left column, then look to the right to see the correlation to other investments. Note that the same investment would have a correlation of 1.00 (i.e., managed futures have a 1.00 correlation to managed futures).

Observations of Figure 8.4 lead to some conclusions that indicate a possible opportunity to diversify:

	Managed Futures	Global Macro	Long/Short Equity	U.S. Stocks	U.S. Bonds
Managed Futures	1.00	0.52	-0.01	-0.16	0.24
Global Macro	0.52	1.00	0.72	0.45	0.17
Long/Short Equity	-0.01	0.72	1.00	0.76	-0.02
U.S. Stocks	-0.16	0.45	0.76	1.00	-0.03
U.S. Bonds	0.24	0.17	-0.02	-0.03	1.00

FIGURE 8.4: Correlation Table, January 1997–March 2012
Source: Altegris
Past performance is not indicative of future results. The referenced indices are shown for general market comparisons and are not meant to represent any particular fund. An investor cannot invest directly in an index. Moreover, indices do not reflect commissions or fees that may be charged to an investment product based on an index, which may materially affect the performance data presented. There is no guarantee an investment will achieve its objective, generate profits, or avoid losses. Managed Futures: Altegris 40 Index®; Long/Short Equity: HFRI Equity Hedge (Total) Index; Global Macro: Barclay Global Macro Index; U.S. Stocks: S&P 500 TR Index; U.S. Bonds: Barclay U.S. Aggregate Composite Bond Index.

- Managed futures[57] have been noncorrelated to U.S. stocks and long/short equity. Furthermore, they have had a low correlation to U.S. bonds.

- Global macro has had a moderate level of correlation with managed futures and U.S. stocks and a low correlation with U.S. bonds.

- Long/short equity has been noncorrelated to U.S. bonds and moderate to highly correlated to U.S. stocks.

In addition to having low-to-moderate correlations with stocks and bonds (diversification), these strategies have had historical lower volatility and better performance (than U.S. stocks) over the past 15 years (See Figure 8.5). Of course, and as mentioned before, past performance is not indicative of future returns.

Like all investments, many risks are associated with alternative investments. Ultimately, it is up to you to either rely on competent guidance from your financial advisor or research an investment to understand the risks. This research[58] should include, at a minimum:

- Read a fund's prospectus and related materials. Make sure you understand the level of risk involved in the fund's investment strategies, and then determine whether the risks are suitable to your personal investing goals, time horizons, and risk tolerance. As with any investment, the higher the potential returns, the higher the risks, you must assume.

- Understand how fund assets are valued. Hedge funds may hold investments that are difficult to sell and may be difficult to value. You should understand the valuation process and know the

---

[57] Futures trading is speculative, involves substantial risk, and is not suitable for all investors. Risks include the following: there is the potential loss of your total investment; the funds are highly leveraged; your investment could be illiquid; performance is expected to be volatile; an investment in the fund may not diversify an overall portfolio; and increased competition from other trend-following traders could reduce the fund's profitability.

[58] U.S. Securities and Exchange Commission.

	Annual Rate of Return	Annual Standard Deviation	Worst Drawdown	Sharpe Ratio
Managed Futures	6.72%	10.59%	−13.24%	0.43
Global Macro	9.02%	6.11%	−6.42%	1.04
Long/Short Equity	9.12%	9.89%	−30.59%	0.68
U.S. Stocks	6.18%	16.53%	−50.95%	0.30
U.S. Bonds	6.24%	3.55%	−3.82%	1.03

FIGURE 8.5: Performance Table, January 1997–March 2012
Managed futures, global macro and equity long/short are favorable to traditional asset classes on a risk-return basis and are largely uncorrelated as well.
Source: Altegris
Past performance is not indicative of future results. The referenced indices are shown for general market comparisons and are not meant to represent any particular fund. An investor cannot invest directly in an index. Moreover, indices do not reflect commissions or fees that may be charged to an investment product based on an index, which may materially affect the performance data presented. There is no guarantee an investment will achieve its objective, generate profits or avoid losses. Managed Futures: Altegris 40 Index®; Long/Short Equity: HFRI Equity Hedge (Total) Index; Global Macro: Barclay Global Macro Index; US Stocks: S&P 500 TR Index; US Bonds: Barclay US Aggregate Composite Bond Index. Standard deviation is a statistical measure of how consistent returns are over time; a lower standard deviation indicates historically less volatility. Drawdown measures the peak-to-valley loss relative to the peak for a stated time period. Sharpe ratio measures return in excess of the risk-free rate, per unit of risk, as measured by standard deviation. Date range based on common period of data availability for shown indices.

extent to which a fund's holdings are valued by independent sources.

- Understand fees. Fees impact your return on investment. Most hedge funds typically charge an asset management fee of 1–2 percent of assets, plus a "performance fee" of 20 percent of the hedge fund's profit. A performance fee could motivate a hedge fund manager to take greater risks in the hope of generating a larger return.

- Understand any limitations, including fees, expenses, or charges, on your right to redeem your shares. Hedge funds typically limit opportunities to redeem, or cash in, your shares, to four times a year or less, and often impose a "lock-up" period of one year or more, during which you cannot cash in your shares.

- Research hedge fund managers. Make sure hedge fund managers are qualified to manage your money, and find out whether they have a disciplinary history within the securities industry. You can get this information by reviewing the adviser's Form ADV, which is the investment adviser's registration form. You can search for and view a firm's Form ADV using the SEC's Investment Adviser Public Disclosure (IAPD) website. If you don't find the investment adviser firm in the SEC's IAPD database, call your state securities regulator or search FINRA's BrokerCheck database.

- Ask questions. You are entrusting your money to someone else. You should know where your money is going, who is managing it, how it is being invested, and how you can get it back. In addition, you may wish to read FINRA's investor alert, which describes some of the risks of investing in funds of hedge funds.

At this point, you may be saying, "So, Gary, are you telling me that alternative investments, such as global macro, managed futures, and long/short might have the potential to reduce my risk and increase my return?" And my answer would be, "Yes." Let's look at another alternative investment to solidify the point further.

As you see in Figure 8.6, the private equity benchmark, as represented by the Thomson Reuters data, over the measured period, performed better than the S&P 500 Index with less volatility. In addition to historically higher risk-adjusted returns, private equity typically has demonstrated a low correlation with traditional stock and bond investments. Private equity does have unique risks to consider as well;[59]

- Limited marketability and transferability
- Illiquidity

---

[59] *http://www.hsbcprivatebankfrance.com/english/Benefits-risks-Private-Equity.asp*

Why Invest in Private Equity?
Private Equity vs. S&P 500:
15+ Year Performance Comparison

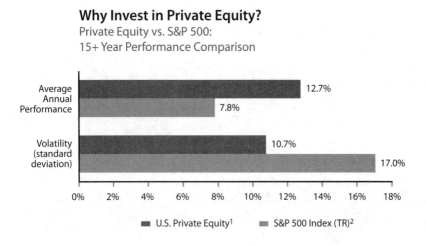

Private equity offers the potential for outperformance of public markets

Figure 8.6: Private Equity
Source: Thomson Reuters
Note: **Past Performance is not indicative of future results**. The private equity benchmark returns are for illustrative purposes only and do not represent any actual portfolio.
[1]Private Equity data from Thomson Reuters (cash flow summay report) 1/1/1993–12/31/2011 with annualized figures based on quaterly data; performance calculated as time weighted return net of underlying fund fees. Thomson Reuters is a standard benchmark for the private equity industry.
[2]Source: S&P 500 total return data from Bloomberg 1/1/1993–12/31/2011; performance calculated based on compound quarterly growth rates.

- Complex tax considerations
- Lack of regulatory oversight
- Delayed or limited valuation

   We could continue discussing the benefits and risks of real estate, natural resources, and other alternative investments, but such a discussion would lead to similar results—adding alternatives could potentially reduce your volatility and increase your returns over a long period of time. The purpose of the previous discussion is not to turn you into a hedge fund manager or to become an expert on alternative investments.

I simply wanted to scratch the surface and show you strategies you may want to research further, either with your financial advisor's assistance or through your own research initiatives.

Let's pull this together and show you how it might work in the following illustration. As you see in Figure 8.7, by adding alternative investments to the traditional balanced portfolio, performance could have increased from 6.2 percent each year to 7.30 percent each year, during

> **Key Point:** *Alternative investments have the potential to benefit your portfolio by managing risk through diversification. Understanding the benefits and risks of the various types of alternatives is an arduous task, but might be a profitable endeavor.*

The Potential Benefits of Adding Alternatives to Traditional Balanced Portfolios
Illustrative Portfolio Data Comparison

Portfolio Data: January 1997–December 2011

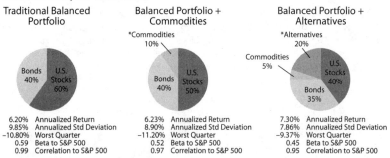

Traditional Balanced Portfolio	Balanced Portfolio + Commodities	Balanced Portfolio + Alternatives
6.20% Annualized Return	6.23% Annualized Return	7.30% Annualized Return
9.85% Annualized Std Deviation	8.90% Annualized Std Deviation	7.86% Annualized Std Deviation
–10.80% Worst Quarter	–11.20% Worst Quarter	–9.37% Worst Quarter
0.59 Beta to S&P 500	0.52 Beta to S&P 500	0.45 Beta to S&P 500
0.99 Correlation to S&P 500	0.97 Correlation to S&P 500	0.95 Correlation to S&P 500

FIGURE 8.7: Alternatives Have the Potential to Increase Returns and Reduce Risk

The above is shown for comparative purposes only and should not be construed as investment advice. PAST PERFORMANCE IS NOT NECESSARILY INDICATIVE OF FUTURE RESULTS. An investor cannot invest directly in an index. Moreover, indices do not reflect commissions or fees that may be charged to an investment product based on the index, which may materially affect the performance data presented. Alternatives composed of equally weighted Morningstar Hedge Fund Categories: Equity Market Neutral, Global Long/Short Equity, Global Macro, Long/Short Debt, Multi-strategy, Systematic Futures and Cambridge Associates Indices: U.S. Private Equity and U.S. Venture Capital. Commodities composed of the Dow Jones UBS Commodity TR Index. Bonds composed of the Barclays Aggregate Bond TR Index. U.S. Stocks composed of the S&P 500 TR Index.

the 14-year period for the blended portfolio with alternatives. Furthermore, the risk of the portfolio measured by standard deviation could have decreased by 20 percent, from 9.85 percent to 7.86 percent!

If you are already using alternative investments, it is my hope that this information confirms your decision. If you are not, you may be saying, "How do I access them?" Hedge funds and private investments typically require an investor to have a certain level of sophistication and net worth in order to invest in the partnership or investment. The Securities and Exchange Commission defines this sophistication as an "accredited" investor. Some investments may require you to be a qualified client or qualified purchaser. I have included definitions of each of these in the Disclosures and Definition section at the back of this book.

Don't worry if you don't meet the criteria for accredited investor, qualified purchaser, or qualified client. With the vast amount of alternative investment mutual funds, exchange-traded products, and publicly traded partnerships available in today's marketplace, you will have plenty of access to hedge fund and private investment-style investments, if they are right for you.

> **Key Point:** *Researching alternative investments requires either a competent financial advisor who is experienced in such investments or a significant commitment of your time.*

MONEY MARKET FUNDS

In today's low-interest-rate environment, money market funds[60] are unlikely to be a core holding. Assuming a low-interest-rate environment, you will find that money market funds in a portfolio may have two benefits:

1. Money market funds can be used to take advantage of market dips by buying after a market correction or a decrease in the market.

---

[60] An investment in money market funds is not insured or guaranteed by the FDIC or any other government agency. Although money market funds seek to preserve the value of your investment at $1.00 per share, it is possible to lose money by investing in money market funds.

2. Money market funds can be used as a "holding account" to collect dividends and interest if you are taking withdrawals from the account. You can set up a systematic withdrawal to provide for your monthly income needs instead of liquidating holdings on a monthly basis. My suggestion is to keep three to twelve months of this systematic withdrawal amount in money market funds and then set up a "electronic funds transfer" to your checking account.

Step 4: Monitor Your Investments.

Having a process to monitor your portfolio is important and often overlooked. It entails reviewing your investments to make sure they still are performing as you expected. You will need to determine the frequency of your reviews (i.e., daily, weekly, monthly, annually) and what you will review at each frequency.

When you do your review, you may find that you need to rebalance. We discussed rebalancing at length on pages 143–145, but it's important to mention once again that rebalancing your portfolio is an important step in the monitoring process. Without rebalancing, your portfolio is likely to become more risky than you intended. You will also need to review the investments that you currently own to make sure they are still the best available. New investments are being manufactured regularly; staying abreast of new products is vital. Comparing your current holdings to potential new investments will allow you to confirm that your investments are still "best-in-class."

Step 5: Document Your Process.

I wouldn't necessarily consider this a "step" but more of an ongoing process. When you have finished building your portfolio, you should have a written process that explains your procedures for asset allocation and investment selection. In fact, your documentation should be happening as you make decisions in each step of the process. You may ask why documentation is important. Trying to remember why you decided to reduce an asset class from the prescribed asset allocation percentage a year after you made that decision will prove difficult. However, if you write it down, you will be in good shape and probably have one of those aha moments.

APPLYING THE FINISHING TOUCHES

Unlike art, the process of managing an investment portfolio is never complete. You can't put the finishing touches on it and put it in a frame to observe. It never gets a frame. It is a painting that never dries. You will always be adding finishing touches.

You may have to change colors, or investment products, over time. The background, or economic climate, will evolve and cause you to make adjustments. Your risk capacity may decrease over time, turning your masterpiece from a contemporary to a more traditional work of art. Just like an artist mastering his or her skills, it is difficult to learn about investing from a few chapters in a book. As an artist is dedicated to performance, an investor is dedicated to his or her portfolio. Patience and conviction, especially while out-of-favor investments are underperforming, are requirements to being a successful investor.

As with art, creativity is sometimes required when managing investments. Determining the best ways to generate income—creating the cash flow from your masterpiece—can be accomplished in numerous ways. There is no right or wrong way, and experience and education will surely be important.

Think about this:

> *We sometimes forget that investing is a means to an end, but not an end in itself. The means is making money, but the end is freedom and security for ourselves and our families. In other words, it's not whether you beat an index, it's whether you can afford life goals, such as sending your kids to college, having a comfortable retirement, and leaving a legacy to future generations.*

I hope this chapter, as well as the previous two chapters, has made you think, opening your mind to possible considerations to turn your investment portfolio into a masterpiece.

9 | The Artist Within?

"Genius is eternal patience."

—Michelangelo

Although Michelangelo surely had assistance with the painting of the Sistine Chapel, many of his works of art were completed with only his hands. He had confidence in his abilities and skill. He was a master of the tools available to him—paints, chisels, hammers, brushes. He had the desire, even without the support of his father, to follow his dream and become one of the greatest artists to ever live.

Besides his natural skills, he studied and served as an apprentice to sharpen his abilities. At age 13, Michelangelo was apprenticed to the painter Domenico Ghirlandaio whose masterpieces include *The Last Supper*. From 1490 to 1492, Michelangelo attended the humanist academy, founded by the Medici family along neo-Platonic lines, and studied sculpture under Bertoldo di Giovanni. Becoming a master required not only his natural artistic ability, but also a desire and patience in conjunction with a work ethic and study.

Financial planning and investment management do not require that you are born with an inherent artistic skill set like it does an artist or musician, but it will require other qualities that Michelangelo attained. Specifically, it requires the desire to learn and patience. It also requires you to have a temperament that allows you to be objective.

As you create your masterpiece, you will need to look introspectively at yourself and determine whether you have the desire, propensity, and temperament to do the following:

- Determine what are your goals and how to articulate them.
- Create a financial plan that incorporates your goals with their financial costs.
- Implement your plan using the tools and resources available.
- Control the direction of your plan and make changes as life evolves.
- Throw off discouragement and manage your emotions.

THE THREE TS: TIME, TRAINING, AND TEMPERAMENT

If you are reading this book, you most likely fall into one of three categories:

1. You have a financial advisor and are happy with the services provided.
2. You do your own financial planning and investment management.
3. You have a financial advisor and you are *considering* doing your own financial planning and investment management.

This section of the book will address #2 and #3 in the preceding list. In order to manage your own finances, I believe three components determine your success: time, training, and temperament.

Time

In order to effectively manage your own finances, you need to honestly answer this question: Do you have the time needed to plan, research, and monitor your investments, as well as to update your financial plan as life changes? In order to answer this question, you will need to know how much time is required to perform these tasks. Unfortunately, the question has no simple answer. The time needed depends on a number of factors, including:

- How complicated is your financial situation?
- Based on your aptitude, how much time will it take you to study and understand the software and other tools needed to create your financial plan and research your investments?

Getting started with the creation of a financial plan can be a time-consuming process. You will need to become familiar with the software and spend time inputting the data to effectively run the analysis. Your planning software may be simple or complicated; among the many choices, and depending on your situation, selecting the most appropriate software is vital. The program may be as simple as inputting age, retirement age, assets accumulated thus far, level of ongoing regular saving, and return and inflation projections. Or it could be significantly more complex, including the inclusion of tax rates (now and projections for the future) for both income and capital gains and asset classes. It may also ask you to include different what-if scenarios such as the following:

- If you are married and one spouse dies prematurely, would the surviving spouse pay off any debts?
- Do you plan on staying in your current residence during retirement or downsizing? What assumptions will be made regarding the equity in your existing home and growth rate of the value of the home?
- Do you plan on working part time in retirement? For how long? For how much income?
- Will your expenses vary in retirement? You may want to travel or participate in more expensive hobbies during the early part of your retirement and reduce expenses in your later years.
- Will you include the potential impact of an inheritance?
- Should you include additional expenses for long-term care insurance?

These questions cover just a few of the potential issues that may need to be addressed in your financial plan. Questions like these fall into three different categories. Setting politics aside, Donald Rumsfeld (the thirteenth and twenty-first U.S. Secretary of Defense) said it best:

> *As we know, there are known knowns. There are things we know we know. We also know there are known unknowns. That is to say we know there are some things we do not know. But there are also unknown unknowns, the ones we don't know we don't know.*

Trying to capture as many of the "known knowns" in the financial plan is important because, even with the best planning tools and assumptions, we will all encounter many "known unknowns" and "unknown unknowns."

Once you have your financial plan in place and understand the resources needed to achieve your goals, you will then need to review the resources you have available to determine whether you are on track to reach those goals (i.e., are you saving enough, or have you saved enough?).

From there, you will need time to determine your asset allocation and select appropriate investments. On an ongoing basis, you will need to have a system to monitor the investments you selected and compare them to other investments to ensure they are still meeting your criteria.

As we know, each day holds a finite amount of time. How you spend those hours is simply a matter of what matters the most to you. After factoring in the parts of the day that are necessary, such as sleeping, eating, and possibly working, you then need to think about the other waking hours. Do you have the time you desire to spend with your family and friends, possibly participate in community and faith-based activities, and exercise? Are you willing to reduce time in those or other important activities to research and monitor your investments?

You may be saying to yourself, "I don't need to spend that much time on my investment portfolio or planning." Or you may be saying,

"I have been managing my own finances for years, and I've never had to sacrifice any other activities." Yes, your assessment may be true, but if you have made these statements, you need to ask yourself, "Is there something that I don't know that I should be doing that I am not currently doing?" I have always been fond of the saying, "You don't know what you don't know."

> **Key Point:** *Time is a valuable and finite resource. Like exercising, you have to be willing to commit the time needed to plan your finances.*

Training

You don't have to be a rocket scientist to do your own financial planning, but you do need more than a basic knowledge of investing to manage your own portfolio. How *much* knowledge needed is subjective.

Do you need to read 10 books on investing and financial planning to be able to make good decisions with your money? Do you need to take a class? Or do you need to read (and understand!) the 616-page book, *Security Analysis,* by Benjamin Graham and David Dodd? Do you need to know the definitions of every risk measure and how to perform technical analysis on a security? As you can see, determining when you are adequately prepared to manage your own finances can only be determined by you. You need to have the confidence that you know what you need to know.

Ultimately, you have to decide how much formal education you will need to manage your wealth alone. You also need to make sure that, as new products and technologies arrive, you review them and, if appropriate, add them to your repertoire of resources.

> **Key Point:** *The training necessary to manage your own finances is subjective and, ultimately, determined by you.*

Temperament

In my opinion, the most challenging part of managing one's own finances is temperament. Do you have the patience, confidence, conviction, and ability to throw off discouragement while your investments fluctuate?

If you have the time, dedication, and propensity to learn, you can study enough material to become an expert in financial theory and investment due diligence. However, learning how to control your emotions while making objective decisions with your investments is a skill that may be difficult to learn. Will you be able to sell an investment if it has gone up substantially when your analysis or target allocation suggests you sell? If an investment that still meets your criteria drops substantially in value, are you able to objectively purchase more of that investment in order to "buy low"?

> **Key Point:** *Managing your emotions while investing is just as important as the analysis required for selecting an investment.*

TRUST IN OTHERS

If you decide that you don't have the time, training (or willingness to learn), and/or temperament needed to manage your own finances, you will need to place your trust with someone who can assist you.

For some people, taking this step is difficult. Some believe they are giving up control. Others have a hard time trusting others, especially when it comes to financial matters. Can you trust someone to handle your finances? Do you want to be an active participant in the investment decisions or completely pass the day-to-day management to a professional?

EVERY PIECE OF ART IS UNIQUE

Everyone's situation is unique. This uniqueness requires the discussion of risk, investments, goals, personality, emotions, lifestyle, and how we value money. Artwork is similar; every *piece* of art is unique. Wouldn't it be nice if retirement planning was like a paint-by-numbers picture of *Mona Lisa*? We could all just use the same investment and save the same amount of money as everyone else. We would not have to worry about the economy or our investment portfolio. We would simply use the same "colors" as everyone else and know that we had a perfect masterpiece. Unfortunately, paint-by-colors does not describe the situation. Generally speaking, even though we may have the same resources as everyone else, how we use those resources is limited by our intelligence, availability, and understanding.

Michelangelo, using his knowledge of carving, created the statue of *David*. He understood through his knowledge of carving how various tools would affect the stone. At the same time, he knew that he needed to be precise. A mistake, such as hammering off too much stone, would permanently ruin his masterpiece. While planning and investing requires precision too, some mistakes may be forgiven. Unfortunately though, some mistakes may not. For those investors who invested all of their money in technology stocks right before the bubble burst in 2000, well, that type of mistake will be felt for decades to come, as we now know.

So, as you contemplate your desire to manage your finances, consider the following:

- The time you have and are willing to spend on these matters. Do you have the time, when taking into consideration other parts of life that are important to you?
- The resources you have access to—books, research, software, etc.
- Your own temperament. Can you be objective with your own money?

10 | Like Art, Advisors Are Unique Too

"I am still learning."

—Michelangelo

MICHELANGELO RECEIVED ART TRAINING FROM ITALIAN RENAISSANCE painter Domenico Ghirlandaio and sculpting training from Renaissance sculptor Bertoldo di Giovanni, two of the greatest artists of his time. They trained him to hone his craft and taught him the fine details of painting and sculpture. But what if Michelangelo didn't learn from those particular mentors? How would that have affected the art he created? Chances are that his works of art would look different.

Just as *art* is one of kind, humans are too. We have different looks, education, experiences in life, personalities, emotions, and so on. This chapter is about how to select a competent financial advisor, which means finding the right person, out of thousands of professionals, to assist you with your finances.

As I began writing this chapter, I thought it would be the easiest one to write. In fact, it is proving to be the toughest. Selecting a financial advisor is similar in many ways to finding a partner in life. It is a special relationship, one that should be cherished. That may sound hokey, but I believe it is true. It is not the same kind of relationship you would have with other professionals, such as your attorney or tax advisor. Those relationships are important and can last for a lifetime, but your relationship with your financial advisor will have more emotional and psychological components. It will involve the emotions that occur when you reach your goals—when you are able to retire comfortably or send your children to college—because you had the resources available. It could involve the emotions that are an inherent part of investing—how you feel when your investments gain or lose value.

In some respects, finding your life partner or spouse is *easier* than finding a financial advisor. The process of dating different people, sometimes over a course of years, allows you to get to know that person well. However, when you are interviewing the person who is going to manage your wealth, you may only have a few hours to determine whether this person is right for you. To make the most out of the time you spend with your prospective *financial* partner, I hope this chapter will provide you with the knowledge you need to help you find your perfect match.

When determining whether a financial advisor is the one for you, you need to consider many elements. Like Michelangelo's mentors were to him, a financial advisor has the opportunity to be a meaningful part of your life. But because every financial advisor has a different personality, investment philosophy, and education, it can be an overwhelming decision. However, we are going to break down the decision-making process into a more systematic process. Although someone's personality traits are hard to quantify, some facets of a financial advisor can easily be compared to those of other advisors. We will focus on both the easily quantifiable characteristics, as well as the harder-to-determine personality factors.

As you read this chapter, you may currently find yourself in one of four different situations:

1. You may be doing your own financial planning and investment management. You may be satisfied with your progress and abilities. Therefore, you may conclude you do not need the assistance of a financial advisor/planner.

2. You may be doing your own financial planning and investment management, but you feel like your results and planning can benefit from working with a professional.

3. You may currently have a financial advisor and are happy with the services and relationship. I hope a review of this information will increase the confidence you have in your relationship.

4. You may be working with a financial advisor, but are not happy with the services and/or relationship. You are considering making a change.

So, if you are in situations #2 or #4 and want to know how to select a financial professional as an advisor and confidant, we will share all the information you need to make that decision. This chapter will assist you in the process of finding a long-lasting, trust-based relationship that could span decades and possibly continue to the next generation.

EVERY ADVISOR IS DIFFERENT

During the course of my career, hundreds of prospective clients have asked me if I could help them. Some of them are individuals who have never worked with a financial advisor and others would be considered "second opinions." Most of the time, they fall into the latter category.

The meetings are similar in the sense that each prospective client has a portfolio, either created by them or with the help of another advisor. Often, a potential new client will pull out a handful of investment statements and ask the question, "What do you think about my portfolio?" Think about this question for a moment. We are not talking about getting a second opinion as to whether you should have a surgery for an ailment. Much more *art* than science goes into the portfolio question. Why? As you read this chapter, you will learn that every financial advisor is different. More than likely, what one financial advisor believes is the best thing for you will be different from what another financial advisor believes is best for you. I draw the analogy of going into a Ford dealership and asking the salesperson if he or she thinks the Toyota sedan is better than the Ford sedan.

UNDERSTANDING THE "KNOWNS"

When you are deciding which advisor to work with, a few criteria are easy to compare one against another. They include the method of fees, education, experience, qualifications/credentials, and disciplinary actions.

Fees

An advisor charges for his or her services in three main ways. They include fee-only, fee-based, and commission-based. Each has its pros and cons, and none are right or wrong in and of themselves. The important part is understanding the differences so you are comfortable with your advisor's method of compensation.

Fee-Only: This advisor is paid a flat fee, an hourly rate, and/or a percentage of the investments they manage on your behalf. Typically, this advisor will have discretion over the portfolio, which means that advisor will buy and sell based on his or her understanding of managing a portfolio. The advisor is paid a fee, which typically means less opportunity for a conflict of interest. For example, if an advisor charges 1 percent on assets under management (typical fees range from 0.50% to 2.00% depending on the size of the portfolio), then the advisor makes more money when your account does well. Conversely, if your account does poorly, the advisor makes less money (but still earns a fee on the lesser portfolio value).

This type of arrangement typically allows a financial advisor the opportunity to invest in many different types of investment vehicles, such as mutual funds, exchange-traded funds, separately managed accounts, individual bonds and stocks, hedge funds, and private equity without the potential conflict of investing in a product because it has a high commission. Investments that are inherently commission-based investments, such as non-listed REITS (real estate investment trusts), are generally not available to invest in with this type of platform. A possible conflict of interest exists when you have potential investments outside the scope of the advisor (such as paying off a mortgage) that would reduce the amount of money that the advisor manages. Another possible conflict could be when an advisor who charges by the hour, racks up billable hours; you should be given a detailed breakdown of the number of hours charged and what was done during that time.

Fee-based: This approach is also known as a combination fee and commission structure. You are charged a fee for some services, but might also pay a commission on the purchase of certain products. Examples of commission-based products include insurance and certain investments such as load-based mutual funds, most annuities, or simply a transaction of buying a stock.

Sometimes an investment account may be too small (i.e., a Roth IRA that has $5,000 worth of investments) to justify using a fee-based account. Some advisors will manage an account on a fee-basis with as little as $10,000, but most do not. Understanding the limitations of a fee-based account is important.

Commission: This financial advisor is compensated with commissions provided by the product sponsor. The advisor is paid at the time of the transaction and possibly a trailing (ongoing) commission, which could create a possible conflict of interest because the advisor makes money at the time of the sale. Some advisors might select investments that generate more commission for themselves even if a lower-cost option would be equally effective. However, nothing is inherently wrong with commission-based business models. The most important factor is whether the advisor offers a suitable product for the client and also ensures he or she has the client's best interest at heart.

Word of warning: Sometimes a commission-based advisor will provide financial planning services "free of charge." As the saying goes, "Nothing in life is free." Be careful. The advisor may be using financial planning as a loss leader to then recoup his or her time through more expensive products. Of course, this scenario is not always the case, just something to be mindful of.

Education

Does a financial advisor need a college degree in *finance* to be equipped to give you guidance? Of course not. Would it help if they had a business or financial-oriented education? Probably, but I wouldn't put too much weight on this factor. A college degree is a must, but on-the-job experience and training are equally important.

Experience

How many years has the financial advisor been practicing? Like everything else in life, experience matters. This industry, like the technology industry, is evolving rapidly as more investment products become available and economic conditions are dynamic. Ideally, experienced financial advisors will have seen both good and bad market conditions and have a deep knowledge of all products available. They will have guided individuals in situations similar to yours and will understand the challenges and decisions you are facing. Experience cannot be overlooked. On the other hand, do you want to work with someone who has 30 years of experience and is going to retire in five years when you are in your mid-fifties? In this scenario, you will need to make sure that the financial advisor has a succession plan in place that allows you to feel comfortable.

How many years of experience are recommended? That is a tough question. It is partially based on the capacity of the individual giving the advice and not on any magic numbers. It is up to you to discern, with your own intellect, as well as with the factors laid out in this chapter, whether your advisor has enough experience to advise you.

Qualifications/Credentials

According to a regulatory survey by the Investor Protection Trust and reported in *InvestmentNews,* 58 percent of seniors are not able to decipher the legitimacy of designations held by financial planners, advisors, and others working with elders.[61] That is understandable. According to AARP, at least 100 financial designations are in circulation! Check out any professional designation by contacting the issuing organization to determine whether the advisor is currently authorized to use the designation and whether that advisor has been disciplined. Make sure you understand the requirements for a professional designation. The criteria used by organizations that grant professional designations for investment professionals vary greatly. Some require formal certification procedures, including examinations and continuing professional education credits. Others may merely signify that membership dues have been paid—the kind of designation that may not be credible.

In my opinion, here are the most important designations for financial advisors to hold. They show a depth of experience and skill. Some advisors may hold one or more designations.

CFP®–A CERTIFIED FINANCIAL PLANNER™ Professional. As of the time of this writing, about 32,853 advisors have this credential. Advisors and planners are certified after meeting extensive educational requirements by the College for Financial Planning or another approved educational program. A bachelor's degree, examination, and experience requirements must also be met. All graduates must complete continuing education (CE) requirements, an ethics update, and pay a license fee to maintain this designation.

CIMA®–Certified Investment Management Analyst. This designation of the Investment Management Consultants Association is awarded to investment consultants (advisors)—fee-based advisors,

---

[61] *http://www.investmentnews.com/article/20120815/FREE/120819940*

financial managers, investment counsel, and trust officers—who complete educational, examination, and experience requirements. Continuing education (CE) is also required. This well-organized association gives classes at the Wharton School of Business.

CFA® – Chartered Financial Analyst. This designation is offered by the CFA Institute (formerly the Association for Investment Management and Research [AIMR]). To obtain the CFA charter, candidates must successfully complete three difficult exams and gain at least three years of qualifying work experience, among other requirements. In passing these exams, candidates demonstrate their competence, integrity, and extensive knowledge in accounting, ethical and professional standards, economics, portfolio management, and security analysis. CFA charterholders tend to be analysts who work in the field of institutional money management and stock analysis. These professionals provide research and ratings on various forms of investments.

ChFC® – Chartered Financial Consultant. This designation is designed for financial professionals who want to become well versed with the advanced financial planning needs of individuals, professionals, and small business owners. The designation provides in-depth coverage of the key financial planning disciplines, including insurance, income taxation, retirement planning, investments, and estate planning.

CLU® – Chartered Life Underwriter. Insurance or financial specialists who have met work experience and education requirements can receive this designation. They must have completed an educational program offered by The American College, passed 10 examinations covering the application of life and health insurance in filling needs for survivor income, estate planning, business continuation, and employee benefits. They must also have met experience and ethical standards and continuing education requirements of 15 hours yearly.

Disciplinary Actions

If you are working with a U.S. Securities and Exchange Commission (SEC) or state securities agency Registered Investment Adviser (see Big vs. Boutique section), you can review their Form ADV, which they are required to provide to you. They must file this form with either the SEC or the state securities agency in the state where they have their principal place of business. Whether an adviser is regulated by the SEC or state depends on the amount of assets they manage. You can also get copies of this document by accessing the Investment Advisor Public Disclosure (IAPD) website at http://www.advisorinfo.sec.gov. Additionally, you can get in touch with your state securities regulator through the North American Securities Administrators Association (NASAA) website http://www .nasaa.org or by calling (202) 737-0900. Simply ask your state securities regulator whether it has had any complaints about the adviser.

If you are working with an independent financial advisor (affiliated with a broker/dealer) or a stockbroker (affiliated with a major brokerage firm, i.e., UBS, Morgan Stanley, Merrill Lynch) both are regulated by the Financial Industry Regulatory Association (FINRA). You should check the Central Registration Depository (CRD) to look for complaints about any financial advisor working as independently or working for a broker/dealer affiliate. If you find any complaints, you may want to discuss them with him or her. For more information, visit http://www .finra.org/Investors/ToolsCalculators/BrokerCheck/index.htm.

THE RIGHT "FIT"

In addition to the more easily determined considerations already mentioned, you will need to agree more fundamentally with certain other factors, including investment philosophy, personality, and the advisor's business model.

Investment Philosophy

Remember, you are paying your financial advisor for their expertise; therefore, it is not necessary to understand the minutiae to become an expert yourself. Although I don't believe it is necessary to find out each piece of criteria your advisor reviews to select an investment, you may want to understand what tools and research programs he or she has available to use. In order to gain a comfort level with the advisor's resources, you should ask questions, such as the following:

- Do you rely on third-party asset management firms to manage your client's assets or do you manage them internally?
- What types of research programs do you have access to? Is the research proprietary for certain products or is it completely independent, allowing you to look at the entire investment universe?
- How do you determine a client's investment diversification?

The goal of these and other questions is not to necessarily understand the advisor's entire methodology, but instead, to gain confidence that he or she has a system and structure to the approach used.

One last word of warning: Does the advisor try to time the market and claim being able to on a regular basis with fantastic results? Does the advisor brag about market-beating results year after year? If so, get up and walk out.

Personality

Here is where your experience in dealing with people is going to come into play. You need to spend a few hours with this individual before you decide whether you want to work with this advisor. You might really "click" with this person and feel comfortable after having had a few conversations. Remember, it may be the beginning of a lifelong relationship. It is worth the time and research to find someone who gives you a sense of confidence in his or her abilities while also making you feel at ease. Remember the saying: "Business is first a meeting of the hearts and then a meeting of the minds."

Big vs. Boutique

Of the two different types of financial advisors, as defined by the body of regulation that oversees their activities, the one you choose to work with depends on your investment needs and preferences. Advisors are either regulated by and under the supervision of the Securities and Exchange Commission (SEC) or the Financial Industry Regulatory Agency (FINRA).

Registered Investment Advisers (RIAs) are typically regulated by the Securities and Exchange Commission (SEC). However, if the RIA has less than $100 million in assets under management (AUM) and has at least five clients in a state, that person would register with that state regulatory agency instead of the SEC. An RIA offers investment advice for a fee and is not paid on the sale or purchase of securities. This advisor is held to a fiduciary standard of care (what is in the best interest of the investor and which also carries a personal liability responsibility).

Advisors regulated by FINRA typically hold what is known in the industry as a Series 7 (or possibly a more limited registration called a Series 6) registration to offer mutual funds, securities, variable annuities, and other risk-based investments. FINRA-regulated advisors can be further distinguished by the type of firm with which they are affiliated. Some are independent advisors affiliated with an independent broker/dealer (e.g., Commonwealth Financial Network, LPL, or Raymond James). Typically, they will own their own firm and rely on their broker/dealer for compliance, licensing, and trading execution, among other things. Others affiliate with larger brokerage firms, such as Bank of America/Merrill Lynch, UBS, Morgan Stanley and Wells Fargo Financial Advisors.

An advisor regulated by FINRA is held to the "suitability" rule (the product is suitable for the investor) instead of the fiduciary standard. Suitability is defined by FINRA as: "A member or an associated person must have a reasonable basis to believe that a recommended transaction or investment strategy involving a security or securities is suitable for the customer, based on the information obtained through the reasonable diligence of the member or associated person to ascertain the customer's investment profile." If you are working with a CERTIFIED FINANCIAL PLANNER™ Professional, who is also registered with FINRA, this advisor would also be held to the fiduciary standards in addition to the suitability standards. Some investors have become disillusioned with the big firm names and prefer the more personal service of an RIA or one who affiliates with an independent broker-dealer. In both cases, they do not answer to anyone except their compliance/legal department and regulators, so they are free to service their clients any compliant way they choose.

So which do you prefer: Main Street or Wall Street? Only your personal financial circumstances, goals, and personality can help determine what type of advisor and firm would suit you best. However, the most important piece to consider is that, no matter which advisor you select or which firm that advisor is with, he or she must earn your trust. Ultimately, you need to feel confident that the advisor will invest your money responsibly and act in your best interest at all times.

HOW TO FIND YOUR PERFECT MATCH

A referral from someone you respect, to an advisor who has "proven" his or her ability, is worth a lot of credence. Start by asking family members, friends, and business associates who they use for their wealth management needs. You can also use the following resources to help you create a list of potential advisors. Ultimately, you should have a narrow list of, say, three advisors to interview.

So what should you do if your friends, family, or business associates do not have a referral or if you need more potential candidates to interview? Here are a few well-respected financial industry trade associations that train and educate advisors. They also offer programs to help investors find competent advisors and financial planners.

Financial Planning Association (FPA)

The Financial Planning Association (FPA®) is a leadership and advocacy organization connecting investors with those who provide professional financial planning. Based in Denver, Colorado, the FPA has nearly 100 chapters throughout the United States representing tens of thousands of members involved in all facets of providing financial planning services. Working in alliance with academic leaders, legislative and regulatory bodies, financial services firms, and consumer interest organizations, the FPA is a resource for the public to find a financial planner who will deliver advice using an ethical, objective, client-centered process. According to AARP ("How to Choose a Financial Planner," March 23, 2012), roughly 70 percent of the FPA's 23,800 members are CERTIFIED FINANCIAL PLANNER™ professionals.

The National Association of Personal Financial Advisors (NAPFA)

Launched in 1983, the association has developed high standards in the field and each advisor must sign and renew a Fiduciary Oath yearly and subscribe to their Code of Ethics. The association provides support and education for more than 2,400 members (at the time of this writing) across the country, and it is governed by a national board and supported by four regional boards.

The CFP Board of Standards

The mission of Certified Financial Planner Board of Standards, Inc. (CFP Board) is to benefit the public by granting the CFP® certification and upholding it as the recognized standard of excellence for competent and ethical personal financial planning.

The FPA, NAPFA, and the CFP Board of Standards offers resources designed to help the public understand the importance of financial planning and the value of objective advice from a financial planner.

THE PROCESS OF SELECTING THE RIGHT ADVISOR

In addition to the aforementioned criteria for selecting an advisor, the interview process should also follow some guidelines. You should ask the advisor some tough questions to make sure he or she is competent and trustworthy, listen carefully to the questions they ask you, and measure your results.

Ask the Tough Questions

I have been advising clients for more than 19 years at the time of writing this book. During this period, out of hundreds of initial meetings with prospective clients, I can count on one hand the number of times I have been asked the most crucial interview questions, which is unfortunate because questions like the following are widely circulated on numerous credentialed websites. In addition to the other criteria discussed in this chapter, the following questions are important ones to ask when you are considering the help of a financial advisor:

1. Can you only recommend a limited number of products or services to me? If so, why?

2. Have you ever been disciplined by any government regulator for unethical or improper conduct or been sued by a client who was not happy with the work you did?

3. Not including me, who else would benefit from the recommendations you make?

4. Do you sell proprietary products (investments manufactured by the company you work for)? If so, do you receive any additional bonus or compensation for selling these products in lieu of other similar products?

5. Who is your typical client? (You want to make sure that they have experience in helping individuals in situations similar to yours.)

6. Can you give me some references? You should contact each of their references and find out if the advisor's service standards mentioned in the meeting(s) match what the client has experienced. Ask about the performance of the reference's accounts. However, be careful here; if the client has only been working with the advisor for a short period of time and that period was when markets have been tumbling, he or she may have experienced less-than-desired results. (You need to be able to understand how your risk tolerance and the reference's risk tolerance may be different.)

7. Do the owners and employees of the firm invest their own wealth alongside that of clients?

Listen to Their Questions

Is the advisor simply asking you about your investments, assets, and income, or does the advisor want to know more about *you?* If he or she is asking you questions solely about your resources, be cautious. This approach could indicate that the advisor might be more interested in making money than in learning about and helping you achieve your goals. On the other hand, if the advisor asks you about your family, your interests, goals, and risk tolerance, he or she is indicating a sincere desire to help *you.*

The advisor should not sound like he or she is reading a script from a television interview. The use of jargon or words you don't understand doesn't necessarily mean that the advisor is smart, thoughtful, or well informed. Take notes and when the advisor has finished speaking, ask him or her to restate the previous information in plain English. Again, if you don't understand what they say, continue to probe to confirm the advisor is not just repeating the words of Warren Buffet or some other seasoned financial expert.

Measuring the Relationship

As time goes by, you should periodically evaluate your client-advisor relationship. The frequency and criteria used to measure your relationship is partially subjective and partially objective.

One way to measure the relationship would be to base it on how your account is performing. Although performance is certainly important, it may not be the sole best-determining factor of the relationship. Let's suppose you started working with your advisor in October 2007, right before the markets started into a downward spiral that ultimately lasted more than 16 months. If you were invested with even a relatively small percentage in stocks, your account was likely worth less than when you handed over your portfolio to your new advisor. Don't get me wrong, performance is important. However, looking at the big picture, including the economy and your progress toward reaching your goals, is also important.

Some questions to ask about your progress may be: Are assets keeping pace with the projections in the financial plan, if one was created? If not, is it because you are not saving the amount determined by your financial plan, or is it a function of poor investment results? Furthermore, if it is a function of poor investment results, is it due to volatile markets or bad investments?

After you have had time to get to know your advisor personally and professionally, do you still feel as comfortable with him or her as when you started working together? Hopefully during this time your trust and confidence in your advisor has increased. If it has not, you perhaps should consider finding a new advisor. One word of caution, you need to ask yourself, "Have I been a *good client?*" Remember, a successful relationship, whether it is an advisor-client, marriage, or a business partnership, requires all the parties involved be good listeners. It also requires that you meet frequently to continue to nurture the relationship. It will require your advisor to proactively contact you, but it will also require you to find time to meet.

PROTECTING YOUR MASTERPIECE

Nobody likes to be taken advantage of in life, business, or love; it is one of the worst feelings. By educating yourself on the criteria to consider when selecting a financial advisor, you should be able to gain confidence and shelter your masterpiece from bad advice.

Just like a downturn in the market or a bad investment can wreak havoc on an investment, vandalism can permanently damage a piece of art. Michelangelo's masterpieces have had some unlucky harm over the years:

- In 1972, a man attacked the *Pietà* with a hammer, damaging the face and neck and breaking off the left forearm. A transparent barrier is now in place to protect the sculpture.

- In 1991, a hammer-wielding man attacked the sculpture, *David*, breaking apart a toe and his left foot.

Why would someone damage these beautiful pieces of art? The same question could be asked, "Why would someone give you bad advice?" The reasons for both are potentially infinite. The point is, you should gain knowledge of the person giving you advice.

After the initial selection of your financial advisor is over, the process does not end there. With any relationship, you have a responsibility to sustain it. The advisor should have a client-service model that proactively contacts you to schedule face-to-face (if located in the same town), telephone, or video conferences. Furthermore, you should find out how often the advisor reviews your accounts and contacts you over and above the regularly scheduled meetings. Also, the advisor should welcome periodic calls and inquiries from you, and respond in a timely fashion. A trust-based relationship should be cherished and nurtured by both the advisor and the client. Remember, you are not looking for a new best friend, but you want someone who is receptive to your questions and concerns and can address them in a professional manner.

Afterword

I FEEL TRULY BLESSED.

While writing this book, I received encouragement and support from my family, colleagues, and friends. I started writing with one goal: to write a book that would raise a lot of money for the causes that are important to me and my wife. As I was writing, I found another purpose to be equally rewarding.

Writing *The Art of Retirement* helped me realize I have the ability to influence the attitudes and contribute to the education of those who read it. To educate someone on the topics presented, such as leaving a legacy of your values, managing investments, selecting a financial advisor, and in general, making the most out of life, is satisfying.

As I was driving home from a Brigance Brigade Foundation board meeting one evening, I thought back to its mission statement that I was honored to help create:

> The mission of the Brigance Brigade Foundation is to equip, encourage and empower people living with ALS (Amyotrophic Lateral Sclerosis); we strive to improve the quality of life for them and their families by providing needed equipment, resource guidance and support services, in addition to funding various research initiatives.

I realized some of the words of the mission statement really applied to what I was trying to accomplish in the book: "... to equip, encourage and empower people." I hope this book helped equip, encourage, and empower you to make good decisions about your retirement planning and outlook on life.

As the mission statement goes on to say, "... providing needed equipment, resource guidance and support services," I again saw the correlation to what I tried to accomplish with this book; I wanted to provide you with an appreciation of the choices you need to consider as you plan for your retirement while also providing guidance and support along the way.

I truly hope you enjoyed the book and have a blessed retirement!

Gary Williams

Disclosures and Definitions

Please consider the investment objectives, risks, charges, and expenses carefully before investing. The prospectus, which contains this and other information about the investment, can be obtained from your financial professional. Be sure to read the prospectus carefully before deciding whether to invest.

60/40 Portfolio

60% S&P 500 Index/40% Barclays Capital U.S. Aggregate Bond Index.

Accredited Investor

Under the Securities Act of 1933, a company that offers or sells its securities must register the securities with the SEC or find an exemption from the registration requirements. The Act provides companies with a number of exemptions. For some of the exemptions, such as rules 505 and 506 of Regulation D, a company may sell its securities to what are known as "accredited investors."

The federal securities laws define the term accredited investor in Rule 501 of Regulation D as:

1. A bank, insurance company, registered investment company, business development company, or small business investment company;

2. An employee benefit plan, within the meaning of the Employee Retirement Income Security Act, if a bank, insurance company, or

registered investment adviser makes the investment decisions, or if the plan has total assets in excess of $5 million;

3. A charitable organization, corporation, or partnership with assets exceeding $5 million;

4. A director, executive officer, or general partner of the company selling the securities;

5. A business in which all the equity owners are accredited investors;

6. A natural person who has individual net worth, or joint net worth with the person's spouse, that exceeds $1 million at the time of the purchase, excluding the value of the primary residence of such person;

7. A natural person with income exceeding $200,000 in each of the two most recent years or joint income with a spouse exceeding $300,000 for those years and a reasonable expectation of the same income level in the current year; or

8. A trust with assets in excess of $5 million, not formed to acquire the securities offered, whose purchases a sophisticated person makes.

Alpha

A measure of performance on a risk-adjusted basis. Alpha is often considered to represent the value that a portfolio manager adds to or subtracts from a fund's return. A positive alpha of 1.0 means the fund has outperformed its benchmark index by 1 percent. Correspondingly, a similar negative alpha would indicate an underperformance of 1 percent.

Alpha, also known as the Jensen Index, permits the comparison of portfolio managers' performance relative to one another, or relative to the market itself. When applying alpha, it's important to compare funds within the same asset class.

Alternative Investments

Alternatives are investments that don't fall into traditional investment categories—namely long-only stocks, bonds, or cash. Alternative investment managers can invest long or short, across multiple asset classes, aren't constrained to an investment style, and aren't entirely dependent on the markets going up to achieve positive results. Investing in alternative investments may not be suitable for all investors and involves special risks, such as risk associated with leveraging the investment, potential adverse market forces, regulatory changes, and potential illiquidity. There is no assurance that the investment objective will be attained.

Asset Allocation

The process of dividing an investment portfolio among different kinds of assets to optimize the risk/reward trade-off based on an individual or institution's specific situation, goals, and time horizon.

Asset allocation programs do not assure a profit or protect against loss in declining markets. No program can guarantee that any objective or goal will be achieved. The models shown in this book are for illustrative use and clients should meet with an advisor to discuss their personal risk tolerance and suitable recommendations.

Asset Classes

A group of investments that have similar characteristics and behavior in the marketplace. Types of asset classes include stocks, bonds, cash, and real estate.

Bank of America Merrill Lynch 3-Month U.S. Treasury Bill Index

The Bank of America Merrill Lynch 3-Month U.S. Treasury Bill Index is an index of short-term U.S. government securities with a remaining term to final maturity of less than three months.

Bank of America Merrill Lynch High Yield Master II Index

An unmanaged index consisting of U.S. dollar–denominated bonds that are rated BB1/BB+ or lower, but not currently in default.

Barclays Aggregate Bond Index

The U.S. Aggregate Bond Index is a broad-based benchmark that measures the investment-grade, U.S. dollar–denominated, fixed-rate taxable bond market, including Treasuries, government-related and corporate securities, MBS (agency fixed-rate and hybrid ARM passthroughs), ABS, and CMBS.

Barclays Capital U.S. Investment-Grade Corporate Index

An unmanaged index consisting of publicly issued U.S. corporate and specified foreign debentures and secured notes that are rated investment grade (Baa3/BBB- or higher) by at least two ratings agencies, have at least one year to final maturity and at least $250 million par amount outstanding.

Barclays Capital U.S. Municipal Bond Index

The Barclays U.S. Municipal Bond Index is an unmanaged index of a broad range of investment-grade municipal bonds that measures the performance of the general municipal bond market.

Barclays Intermediate U.S. Treasury Index

The Barclays Intermediate U.S. Treasury Index includes all publicly issued U.S. Treasury securities that have a remaining maturity of greater than or equal to 1 year and less than 10 years, are rated investment grade, and have $250 million or more of outstanding face value. In addition, the securities must be denominated in U.S. dollars and must be fixed rate and nonconvertible.

Barclays Long-Term U.S. Treasury Index

The Barclays Long-Term U.S. Treasury Index includes all publicly issued U.S. Treasury securities that have a remaining maturity of 10 or more years, are rated investment grade, and have $250 million or more of outstanding face value. In addition, the securities must be denominated in U.S. dollars and must be fixed rate and nonconvertible.

Bear Market

A market in which prices are declining. A market participant who believes prices will move lower is called a "bear." A news item is considered bearish if it is expected to result in lower prices.

Beta

A measure of volatility that reflects the tendency of a security's returns and how the security responds to swings in the markets. A beta of 1 indicates that the security's price will move with the market. A beta of less than 1 means that the security will be less volatile than the market. A beta of greater than 1 indicates that the security's price will be more volatile than the market.

Bonds

Corporate bonds:

Corporate bonds contain elements of both interest rate risk and credit risk. The purchase of bonds is subject to availability and market conditions. The inverse relationship between the price of bonds and the yield means that when price goes up, yield goes down, and vice versa. Market risk is a consideration if sold or redeemed prior to maturity. Some bonds have call features that may affect income.

Municipal bonds:

Municipal bonds are federally tax-free but may be subject to state and local taxes, and interest income may be subject to federal alternative minimum tax (AMT). The purchase of bonds is subject to availability and market conditions. The inverse relationship between the price of bonds and the yield means that when price goes up, yield goes down, and vice versa. Market risk is a consideration if sold or redeemed prior to maturity. Some bonds have call features that may affect income.

Government bonds:

Government bonds are guaranteed only as to timely payment of principal and interest, and, if held to maturity, they offer a fixed rate of return and fixed principal value. Government bonds do not eliminate market risk. The purchase of bonds is subject to availability and market conditions. The inverse relationship between the price of bonds and the yield means that when price goes up, yield goes down, and vice versa. Market risk is a consideration if sold or redeemed prior to maturity. Some bonds have call features that may affect income.

U.S. Treasury bills:

Treasury bills are guaranteed by the U.S. government as to the timely payment of principal and interest, and, if held to maturity, they offer a fixed rate of return and fixed principal value. U.S. Treasury bills do not eliminate market risk. The purchase of bonds is subject to availability and market conditions. The inverse relationship between the price of bills and the yield means that when price goes up, yield goes down, and vice versa. Market risk is a consideration if sold or redeemed prior to maturity.

High-yield/junk bonds:

High-yield/junk bonds invest substantially in lower-rated bonds and are issued by companies without long track records of sales and earnings or by those with questionable credit strength. They carry a greater possibility that adverse changes in the economy or poor performance by the issuers of these bonds may affect the ability to pay principal and interest. High-yield bonds involve substantial risks, tend to be more volatile, and, therefore, may not be suitable for all investors.

Bull Market

A market in which prices are rising. A market participant who believes prices will move higher is called a "bull." A news item is considered bullish if it is expected to result in higher prices.

Cambridge Associates U.S. Private Equity Index

The index is based on returns data compiled on funds representing more than 70 percent of the total dollars raised by U.S. leveraged buy-out, subordinated debt, and special situation managers. Cambridge Associates, LLC, calculates the pooled net time-weighted return by quarter. The pooled means represent the time-weighted rates of return calculated on the aggregate of all cash flows and market values as reported by the general partners to Cambridge Associates. Net returns exclude all management fees, expenses, and performance fees that take the form of a carried interest.

Cambridge Associates LLC U.S. Venture Capital Index

The Cambridge Associates LLC U.S. Venture Capital Index® is an end-to-end calculation based on data compiled from 1,400 U.S. venture capital funds (906 early stage, 150 late and expansion stage, 338 multistage, and 6 venture debt funds), including fully liquidated partnerships, formed between 1981 and 2012 (as of September 30, 2012).

Certificates of Deposit

Certificates of deposits (CDs) typically offer a fixed rate of return if held to maturity, are generally insured by the FDIC or another government agency, and may impose a penalty for early withdrawal.

Commodities

1) A basic good used in commerce that is interchangeable with other commodities of the same type. Commodities are most often used as inputs in the production of other goods or services. The quality of a given commodity may differ slightly, but it is essentially uniform across producers. When they are traded on an exchange, commodities must meet specified minimum standards, also known as a basis grade. 2) Any good exchanged during commerce, which includes goods traded on a commodity exchange.

Investments in commodities may have greater volatility than investments in traditional securities, particularly if the instruments involve leverage. The value of commodity-linked derivative instruments may be affected by changes in overall market movements, commodity index volatility, changes in interest rates, or factors affecting a particular industry or commodity, such as drought, floods, weather, livestock disease, embargoes, tariffs, and international economic, political, and regulatory developments. Use of leveraged commodity-linked derivatives creates an opportunity for increased return but, at the same time, carries the possibility for greater loss.

Correlation

A statistical measure of how two securities move in relation to each other. Correlation is computed into what is known as the correlation coefficient, which ranges between −1 and +1. Perfect positive correlation (a correlation coefficient of +1) implies that as one security moves, either up or down, the other security will move in lockstep, in the same direction. Alternatively, perfect negative correlation means that if one security moves in either direction the security that is perfectly negatively correlated will moves in the opposite direction. If the correlation is 0, the movements of the securities are said to have no correlation; they are completely random.

Distressed Debt

Distressed debt firms specialize in taking over the debt of troubled companies, such as those that are in or on the verge of bankruptcy. They frequently function as private equity firms by forgiving the company's debt in exchange for equity. They often are influential in restructuring or liquidating the company in order to recoup their investment.

Key risks may include:

Credit risk: Bond issuer may not pay.

Asset sale risk: If liquidation is forced, perhaps the assets aren't worth what everyone thought they were worth.

Legal/Bankruptcy court risk: The courts may rule against you and the process takes too long.

Concentration risk: Usually distressed funds/pools of money are concentrated in few positions.

Diversification

A risk management technique that mixes a wide variety of investments within a portfolio. The rationale behind this technique contends that a portfolio of different kinds of investments will, on average, yield higher returns and pose a lower risk than any individual investment found within the portfolio.

Diversification does not assure a profit or protect against loss in declining markets, and diversification cannot guarantee that any objective or goal will be achieved.

Dow Jones-UBS US Commodity Index

An index composed of futures contracts on physical commodities and represents nineteen separate commodities traded on U.S. exchanges, with the exception of aluminum, nickel, and zinc.

Dow Jones US Real Estate Index

The index measures the performance of the real estate industry of the U.S. equity market, including real estate holding and developing and real estate investment trusts (REITs) subsectors.

Efficient Market Hypothesis

The efficient market hypothesis (EMH) asserts that financial markets are "informationally efficient." As a consequence, one cannot consistently achieve returns in excess of average market returns on a risk-adjusted basis, given the information available at the time the investment is made.

Efficient Frontier

A set of optimal portfolios that offers the highest expected return for a defined level of risk or the lowest risk for a given level of expected return. Portfolios that lie below the efficient frontier are suboptimal, because they do not provide enough return for the level of risk. Portfolios that cluster to the right of the efficient frontier are also suboptimal, because they have a higher level of risk for the defined rate of return.

Exchange-Traded Fund

An exchange-traded fund (ETF) is similar to a mutual fund that tracks a specific stock or bond index. ETFs trade on one of the major stock markets and can be bought and sold throughout the trading day, like a stock, at the current market price. And, like stock investing, ETF investing involves principal risk—the chance that you won't get all the money back that you originally invested—market risk, underlying securities risk, and secondary market price.

Fundamental Analysis

A method of evaluating a security that entails attempting to measure its intrinsic value by examining related economic, financial, and other qualitative and quantitative factors.

General Investing

Investments are subject to risk, including the loss of principal. Because investment return and principal value fluctuate, shares may be worth more or less than their original value. Some investments are not suitable for all investors, with no guarantee that any investing goal will be met. Talk to your financial advisor before making any investing decisions.

Government Securities

Guarantees relate only to the prompt payment of principal and interest and do not remove market risks if the investment is sold prior to maturity.

Hedge Funds

Hedge funds are private investment vehicles that manage money for institutions and wealthy individuals. They generally are organized as limited partnerships, with the fund managers as general partners and the investors as limited partners. The general partner may receive a percentage of the assets, additional fees based on performance, or both. Hedge funds originally derived their name from their ability to hedge against a market downturn by selling short. Though they may invest in stocks and bonds, hedge funds are typically considered an alternative asset class because of their ability to implement complex investing strategies that involve many other asset classes and investments.

Hedge funds are not suitable for all investors, because they involve a high degree of risk and are speculative. The risks include, but are not limited to, the following: the funds may be leveraged; investors could lose all or a substantial amount of their investment; higher fees and expenses may be charged, which may increase the risk that returns are reduced; performance can be volatile; the funds are illiquid and there may be restrictions on transferring fund investments; and other specific risks are related to particular funds' investment strategies. Past performance does not guarantee future results. Investors must meet specific suitability standards before investing.

Arbitrage

The nearly simultaneous purchase and sale of securities or foreign exchange in different markets in order to profit from price discrepancies.

Dow Jones Credit Suisse Hedge Fund Index

The Dow Jones Credit Suisse Core Hedge Fund Index is the industry's first asset-weighted, UCITS III–compliant, daily-valued hedge fund index with an unconstrained selection universe. It is unique in that performance reflects that of managed accounts and other regulated fund structures sourced from across a range of platforms. This approach expands the universe for fund selection, allowing for the broadest representation of the liquid hedge fund universe without platform bias. (See http://www.hedgeindex.com/hedgeindex/documents/Dow_Jones_Credit_Suisse_Core_Hedge_Fund_Index-Rulebook_011212.pdf.)

Emerging Markets

Emerging markets (EM) funds invest in countries with developing economies in Eastern Europe, Africa, the Middle East, Latin America, the Far East, and Asia. The largest of which include Brazil, Russia, India, and China ("BRIC" countries). These funds may seek to invest in both long and short positions across a variety of EM asset classes, including equities, interest rates, currencies, and/or credit markets. The potential for rewarding investment opportunities in this category is generally accompanied by relatively high risk. Emerging market investments involve higher risks than investments from developed countries and also involve increased risks due to differences in accounting methods, foreign taxation, political instability, and currency fluctuation.

Equity Market Neutral

Equity market neutral is a hedge fund strategy that seeks to exploit investment opportunities unique to some specific group of stocks while maintaining a neutral exposure to broad groups of stocks defined for example by sector, industry, market capitalization, country, or region.

Event-Driven

Event-driven funds principally invest in the equity and debt securities of companies involved in a wide variety of corporate actions and "special situations." These actions include (but are not limited to) mergers, spin-offs, restructurings, litigations, debt exchanges, shareholder buybacks, proxy contests, security issuance, or other capital structure adjustments. In addition, event-driven funds may invest in companies that are stressed or in various stages of the bankruptcy process.

Key risks may include:

Market risk: Prices may decline.

Industry risk: A particular sector in the economy underperforms.

Leverage risk: Volatility and risk of loss may magnify with use of leverage.

Country/regional risk: World events may adversely affect values.

Global Macro

While managed futures react to trends, global macro managers seek to predict them by anticipating changes in world trade, commodity supply and demand, and currency values. Global macro managers can utilize both fundamental and quantitative approaches to formulate trade ideas. Broad investment themes are typically longer term in nature, but trades can range from intraday to several-year holding periods, depending on the manager's investment strategy and risk/reward profile. The flexible and unrestrictive nature of this investment strategy allows global macro managers to search for profits without regard to borders, economies, or politics.

Key risks may include:

Market risk: Prices may decline.

Leverage risk: Volatility and risk of loss may magnify with use of leverage.

Country/regional risk: World events may adversely affect values.

Long/Short Equity

Long/short equity funds seek to generate equity-like returns that are not dependent on the market going up. These managers take long positions in stocks (buying the stock) that are expected to increase in value and short positions in stocks (selling a borrowed stock) that are expected to decrease in value with a goal of buying it back at a lower price and returning it to a lender. Investment decisions are typically driven by fundamental analysis of individual companies or other securities. Long/short equity funds can be broadly diversified or focused on specific regions, sectors, market capitalizations, or investment styles.

Key risks may include:

Stock market risk: Stock prices may decline.

Industry risk: A particular sector in the economy underperforms.

Leverage risk: Volatility and risk of loss may magnify with use of leverage.

Country/regional risk: World events may adversely affect values.

Long/Short Credit

Long/short credit seeks to take exposure to credit-sensitive securities, long and/or short, based on credit analysis of issuers and securities, and credit market views.

Key risks may include:

Interest rate risk: Bond prices will decline if rates rise.

Credit risk: Bond issuer may not pay.

Income risk: Income may decline.

Leverage risk: Volatility and risk of loss may magnify with use of leverage.

Managed Futures

Managed futures represent an asset class managed by professional money managers, known as Commodity Trading Advisors (CTAs), who use their own trading systems to identify and react to market trends. This trend-following strategy alerts managers when to take long or short positions, giving them the opportunity to potentially profit from both positive and negative developments in multiple markets and asset classes simultaneously. Over the long-term, managed futures have provided investors with strong historical returns and low historical correlation to traditional asset classes. Futures trading is speculative, involves substantial risk, and is not suitable for all investors. Risks include the following: there is the potential loss of your total investment; the funds are highly leveraged; your investment could be illiquid; performance is expected to be volatile; an investment in the fund may not diversify an overall portfolio; and increased competition from other trend-following traders could reduce the fund's profitability.

HFRI RV Fixed Income Corporate Index

HFRI RV Fixed Income Corporate Index includes strategies in which the investment thesis is predicated on realization of a spread between related instruments in which one or multiple components of the spread is a corporate fixed-income instrument. Strategies employ an investment process designed to isolate attractive opportunities between a variety of fixed-income instruments, typically realizing an attractive spread between multiple corporate bonds or between a corporate and risk-free government bond.

HFRI Equity Hedge Index

Funds included in the index include investment managers who maintain positions both long and short in primarily equity and equity-derivative securities. A wide variety of investment processes can be employed to arrive at an investment decision, including both quantitative and fundamental techniques; strategies can be broadly diversified or narrowly focused on specific sectors and can range broadly in terms of levels of net exposure, leverage employed, holding period, concentrations of market capitalizations, and valuation ranges of typical portfolios. Equity hedge managers would typically maintain at least 50 percent, and may in some cases be substantially invested in equities, both long and short.

HFRI Fund of Funds Composite Index

Funds included in the index invest with multiple managers through funds or managed accounts. The strategy designs a diversified portfolio of managers with the objective of significantly lowering the risk (volatility) of investing with an individual manager. The fund of funds manager has discretion in choosing which strategies to invest in for the portfolio. A manager may allocate funds to numerous managers within a single strategy or with numerous managers in multiple strategies. The minimum investment in a fund of funds may be lower than an investment in an individual hedge fund or managed account. The investor has the advantage of diversification among managers and styles with significantly less capital than investing with separate managers.

HFRI Fund Weighted Composite Index

HFRI Fund Weighted Composite Index is an equally weighted performance index of the HFRI hedge fund strategy indices. The HFRI hedge fund strategy indices are broken down into 32 different indices (the fund of funds indices are not included in the HFRI Fund Weighted Composite Index) and are not investable. To be included in this index, the hedge funds must fulfill the following criteria: Report monthly returns to HFRI; report net of all fees returns; report assets in US$. No required asset-size minimum restricts inclusion in the HFRI Fund Weighted Composite Index; the names of the individual hedge funds are not disclosed and there is no requirement for a certain track record length to be part of the index. A fund that does not report any longer will have its past returns kept in the index but will not be used in the future (possible survivorship bias).

Index and Indices

All indices are unmanaged and investors cannot actually invest directly into an index. Unlike investments, indices do not incur management fees, charges, or expenses. Past performance does not guarantee future results.

International

The main risks of international investing are currency fluctuations; differences in accounting methods; foreign taxation; economic, political, or financial instability; lack of timely or reliable information; or unfavorable political or legal developments.

J.P. Morgan EMBI Global Diversified Index

The J.P. Morgan Emerging Market Bond Index Global Diversified Index is a composite index representing an unleveraged investment in emerging market bonds that is broadly based across the spectrum of emerging market bonds and includes reinvestment of income (to represent real assets).

Limited Partnership (LP)

A business organization with one or more general partners, who manage the business and assume legal debts and obligations, and one or more limited partners, who are liable only to the extent of their investments. Limited partnership is the legal structure used by most venture and private equity funds. Limited partners also enjoy rights to the partnership's cash flow, but are not liable for company obligations.

Limited partnerships are subject to special risks, such as potential illiquidity, and may not be suitable for all investors.

Liquidity

Government securities

The investments are subject to market risks, and, if sold prior to anticipated maturity, the value of government securities may be more or less than the investor's original cost.

Bank products

Bank products, such as certificates of deposit and savings accounts, are considered short-term liquid investments. The bank may impose penalties for early withdrawal.

Partnerships

Most limited, private, and real estate trust partnerships should not be described as liquid investments because they have no secondary market. Depending upon the structure of these investments, they also may not be characterized as short-term investments.

London Fix Gold

A price per ounce for gold determined daily at 10:30 and 15:00 GMT by a brief conference call among the five members of the London Gold Pool (Scotia-Mocatta, Barclays Capital, Deutsche Bank, HSBC, and Société Générale). The London spot fix price is the price fixed at the moment when the conference call terminates.

Master Limited Partnership (MLP)

A limited partnership that provides an investor with a direct interest in a group of assets (generally, oil and gas properties). Master limited partnership units trade publicly like stock and thus provide the investor significantly more liquidity than ordinary limited partnerships.

Investing in master limited partnerships (MLPs) entails more company-specific risk than other investments, and proper due diligence and suitability criteria should be observed before investing. MLPs are also subject to general market risk and low energy demand. Risks to MLPs include a slowdown in energy demand, environmental hazards, commodity price fluctuations, and tax law reform. In resource-based MLPs, the resource base eventually runs out unless new assets are acquired. Also, with investors continually searching for yield and the ongoing introduction of new investment products, MLPs may become overbought.

Mean (Geometric) Return

Also called the time-weighted rate of return, a measure of the compound rate of growth of the initial portfolio market value during the evaluation period, assuming that all <u>cash</u> distributions are <u>reinvested</u> in the portfolio. It is computed by taking the geometric average of the portfolio subperiod returns.

Mezzanine Debt

Mezzanine financing occurs when private investors agree to lend money to an established company in exchange for a stake in the company if the debt is not completely repaid on time. It is often used to finance expansion or acquisitions and is typically subordinated to other debt. As a result, from an investor's standpoint, mezzanine financing can be rewarding because the interest paid on the loan can be high.

Key risks may include:

Credit risk: Bond issuer may not pay.

Capital structure risk: The risk that the financial structure of the company could change to the detriment of the debt holder.

Market risk (often times some sort of equity component to go along with the lending): Stock prices may decline.

Interest rate risk: Bond prices will decline if rates rise.

Modern Portfolio Theory

Modern portfolio theory (MPT) states that owning allocations of different asset classes that don't always move up or down together is the best way of maximizing returns while minimizing risk.

Morningstar Hedge Fund Categories

Equity Market Neutral

These funds attempt to reduce systematic risk created by factors such as exposures to sectors, market-cap ranges, investment styles, currencies, and/or countries. They try to achieve this by matching short positions within each area against long positions. These strategies are often managed as beta-neutral, dollar-neutral, or sector-neutral. A distinguishing feature of funds in this category is that they typically have low beta exposures (less than 0.3 in absolute value) to equity market indexes such as the MSCI World. In attempting to reduce systematic risk, these funds put the emphasis on issue selection, with profits dependent on their ability to sell short and buy long the correct securities. ©2012 Morningstar, Inc.

Global Long/Short Equity

These funds primarily take long and short positions in equity securities, but do not fit into any of the other regional categories because they do not have a primary regional focus. At least 75% of the fund's gross exposure is invested in equities. These funds will typically have a beta exposure of greater than 0.3 to a global stock index such as the MSCI World. ©2012 Morningstar, Inc.

Global Macro

These funds base investment decisions on an assessment of the broad macroeconomic environment. They look for investment opportunities by studying such factors as the global economy, government policies, interest rates, inflation, and market trends. As opportunists, these funds are not restricted by asset class and may invest across such disparate assets as global equities, bonds, currencies, derivatives, and commodities. These funds primarily invest through derivatives markets. They typically make discretionary trading decisions rather than using a systematic strategy. At least 60% of the funds' exposure is obtained through derivatives. ©2012 Morningstar, Inc.

Long/Short Debt

These funds primarily take directional positions in global debt. Long and short positions are typically independent of each other. Positions do not fully offset each other, and result in net exposures less than −20% or greater than 20% in a majority of periods. The majority of the funds' assets are invested in debt investments, but the fund manager may also include other instruments. These funds may invest in emerging markets debt, U.S. debt, and global debt, along with credit default swaps. At least 75% of the exposure is tied to fixed-income investments, and short exposure is greater than 20%. ©2012 Morningstar, Inc.

Multistrategy

These funds offer investors exposure to several different hedge fund investment tactics. In most of these cases, all of the assets are managed in-house at the hedge fund, but the assets may be divided between multiple portfolio managers, each of whom focuses on a different strategy. This is not to be confused with a fund of funds, which uses external portfolio managers and strategies, as well as second layer of management and performance fees. An investor's exposure to different tactics may change slightly over time in response to market movements. ©2012 Morningstar, Inc.

Systematic Futures

These funds trade liquid global futures, options, and foreign-exchange contracts largely according to trend-following strategies (such as linking greater than 50% of fund's exposure to such strategies). These strategies are price-driven (technical), and systematic (automated) rather than fundamental or discretionary. Trend followers typically trade in diversified global markets, including commodities, currencies, government bonds, interest rates, and equity indexes. However, some trend followers may concentrate in certain markets, such as interest rates. These strategies prosper when markets demonstrate sustained directional trends, either bullish or bearish. Some systematic futures strategies involve mean-reversion or counter-trend strategies rather than momentum or trend-following strategies. At least 60% of the funds' exposure is obtained through derivatives. ©2012 Morningstar, Inc.

MSCI EAFE Index

The Morgan Stanley Capital International Europe, Australasia, Far East Index is a benchmark of foreign stocks. Compiled by Morgan Stanley, the index is an aggregate of twenty-one individual country indices that collectively represent many of the major markets of the world, including Australia, Austria, Belgium, Denmark, Finland, France, Germany, Greece, Hong Kong, Ireland, Italy, Japan, the Netherlands, New Zealand, Norway, Portugal, Singapore, Spain, Sweden, Switzerland, and the United Kingdom. Most international mutual funds measure their performance against this index. It is a market-capitalization weighted index.

MSCI EM (Emerging Markets)

The MSCI Emerging Markets Index is a free float-adjusted market capitalization index that is designed to measure equity market performance of emerging markets. The MSCI Emerging Markets Index consists of the following twenty-one emerging market country indices: Brazil, Chile, China, Colombia, Czech Republic, Egypt, Hungary, India, Indonesia, Korea, Malaysia, Mexico, Morocco, Peru, Philippines, Poland, Russia, South Africa, Taiwan, Thailand, and Turkey.

MSCI Europe

The MSCI Europe Index is a free float-adjusted market capitalization weighted index that is designed to measure the equity market performance of the developed markets in Europe. The MSCI Europe Index consists of the following sixteen developed market country indices: Austria, Belgium, Denmark, Finland, France, Germany, Greece, Ireland, Italy, the Netherlands, Norway, Portugal, Spain, Sweden, Switzerland, and the United Kingdom.

Natural Resources

Most investments in natural resources such as timber, oil, or natural gas are done through limited partnerships. In some cases, such as timber, the resource replenishes itself; in other cases, such as oil or natural gas, the resource may be depleted over time. Timberland produces income from the trees harvested, but may also grow in value and be converted for use as a real estate development.

Qualified Client[62]

1. A natural person who or a company that immediately after entering into the contract has at least $1 million under the management of the investment adviser;

---

[62] *www.law.uc.edu/CCL/InvAdvRls/rule205-3.html*

2. A natural person who or a company that the investment adviser entering into the contract (and any person acting on his behalf) reasonably believes, immediately prior to entering into the contract, either:

   a. Has a net worth (together, in the case of a natural person, with assets held jointly with a spouse) of more than $2 million at the time the contract is entered into; or

   b. Is a qualified purchaser as defined in section 2(a)(51)(A) of the Investment Company Act of 1940 at the time the contract is entered into; or

3. A natural person who, immediately prior to entering into the contract, is:

   a. An executive officer, director, trustee, general partner, or person serving in a similar capacity, of the investment adviser; or

   b. An employee of the investment adviser (other than an employee performing solely clerical, secretarial or administrative functions with regard to the investment adviser) who, in connection with his or her regular functions or duties, participates in the investment activities of such investment adviser, provided that such employee has been performing such functions and duties for or on behalf of the investment adviser, or substantially similar functions or duties for or on behalf of another company for at least 12 months.

Qualified Purchaser[63]

Any natural person (including any person who holds a joint, community property, or other similar shared ownership interest in an issuer that is excepted under section 3(c)(7) [15 USCS § 80a-3(c)(7)] with that person's qualified purchaser spouse) who owns not less than $5 million in investments, as defined by the Commission;

1. Any company that owns not less than $5 million in investments and that is owned directly or indirectly by or for two or more natural persons who are related as siblings or spouse (including

---

[63] *www.law.uc.edu/CCL/InvCoAct/sec2.html*

former spouses), or direct lineal descendants by birth or adoption, spouses of such persons, the estates of such persons, or foundations, charitable organizations, or trusts established by or for the benefit of such persons;

2. Any trust that is not covered by clause 2 and that was not formed for the specific purpose of acquiring the securities offered, as to which the trustee or other person authorized to make decisions with respect to the trust, and each settlor or other person who has contributed assets to the trust, is a person described in clause 1, 2, or 4; or

3. Any person, acting for its own account or the accounts of other qualified purchasers, who in the aggregate owns and invests on a discretionary basis, not less than $25 million in investments.

Real Estate

Real estate investments make either direct or indirect investments in buildings—either commercial or residential—and/or land. Direct investment involves the purchase, improvement, and/or rental of property; indirect investments are made through an entity that invests in property, such as a real estate investment trust (REIT). Real estate has had a relatively low correlation with the behavior of the stock market and is often viewed as a hedge against inflation. Real estate investments are subject to a high degree of risk because of general economic or local market conditions; changes in supply or demand; competing properties in an area; changes in interest rates; and changes in tax, real estate, environmental, or zoning laws and regulations. REIT units/ shares fluctuate in value and may be redeemed for more or less than the original amount invested.

Price Earnings (P/E) Ratio

The P/E ratio represents the amount investors are willing to pay for each dollar of the firm's earnings. It indicates the degree of confidence investors have in a firm's future performance. It is calculated by dividing the market price per share of common stock by the earnings per share (EPS). Like EPS, the P/E ratio is important to potential investors because it's considered an indicator of how expensive or cheap a stock is. The stocks of faster-growing companies tend to have higher P/E ratios and are often more volatile. A trailing P/E compares the stock price to the previous 12 months of EPS; a forward or leading P/E compares the price to anticipated earnings for the coming year.

Price/Sales Ratio

A company's stock price divided by its per-share revenues for the past 12 months is a ratio often used in combination with other statistics to assess companies relative to their peers, especially those that are in a highly cyclical industry or that are relatively new and do not have meaningful profits.

Private Equity

Like stock shares, private equity represents an ownership interest in a company. However, unlike stocks, private equity investments are not listed or traded on a public market or exchange, and private equity firms often are more directly involved with management of the business than the average shareholder. Private equity often requires a long-term focus before investments begin to produce any meaningful cash flow—if indeed they ever do. Private equity also typically requires a relatively large investment and is available only to qualified investors such as pension funds, institutional investors, and wealthy individuals. Private equity has special and significant risks and is not suitable for all investors.

Growth Capital

A type of private equity investment, most often a minority investment, in relatively mature companies that are looking for capital to expand or restructure operations, enter new markets, or finance a significant acquisition without a change of control of the business.

Buyout

Buyouts occur when private investors—often part of a private equity fund—purchase all or part of a public company and take it private, believing that either the company is undervalued or that they can improve the company's profitability and sell it later at a higher price. In some cases, the private investors are the company's executives, and the buyout is known as a management buyout (MBO). A leveraged buyout (LBO) is financed not only with investor capital but with bonds issued by the private equity group to pay for purchase of the outstanding stock.

Venture Capital

Venture capital funds invest in companies that are in the early to mid-growth stages of their development and may not yet have a meaningful cash flow. In exchange, the venture capital fund receives a stake in the company.

Turnaround

Turnaround is the term used when the poor performance of a company or the business experiences a positive reversal.

Risk-Adjusted Return

A measure of how much money your investment made relative to the amount of risk it took on over a specific time period.

Russell 2000 Index

The index measures the performance of the 2,000 smallest companies in the Russell 3000 Index, which is made up of 3,000 of the biggest U.S. stocks. The Russell 2000 serves as a benchmark for small-cap stocks in the United States.

Sharpe Ratio

The Sharpe ratio was created by Nobel laureate William F. Sharpe and describes how much excess return you are receiving for the extra volatility that you endure for holding a riskier asset. Used to measure how much profit an investor received per unit of risk, the higher the ratio, the better is its risk-adjusted performance. A ratio greater than or equal to one indicates that the return is greater than or proportional to the risk the investor incurred to earn the return. Sharpe Ratio = (Net Return − Risk-Free Rate of Return)/Standard Deviation of the Return.

Remember, you always need to be properly compensated for the additional risk you take for not holding a traditionally lower-risk asset (i.e., Treasury bill). For example, if Manager A generates a return of 10 percent while Manager B generates a return of 8 percent, it would appear that Manager A is a better performer. However, if Manager A, who produced the 10 percent return, took much larger risks than Manager B, it may actually be the case that Manager B has a better risk-adjusted return.

Standard Deviation

Standard deviation is a statistical measure of the consistency of returns over time; a lower standard deviation indicates historically less volatility.

Standard & Poor's (S&P) 500 Index

An index of 500 stocks chosen for market size, liquidity, and industry grouping, among other factors, the S&P 500 is designed to be a leading indicator of U.S. equities and is meant to reflect the risk/return characteristics of the large-cap universe. Companies included in the index are selected by the S&P Index Committee, a team of analysts and economists at Standard & Poor's. The S&P 500 is a market value–weighted index—each stock's weight in the index is proportionate to its market value.

The Standard & Poor's (S&P) Goldman Sachs Commodity Index (GSCI)

The index provides investors with a reliable and publicly available benchmark for investment performance in the commodity markets. It is designed to be tradable, readily accessible to market participants, and cost-efficient to implement. The index is widely recognized as the leading measure of general commodity price movements and inflation in the world economy.

Structured Products

Structured products are complex, illiquid investments whose returns may be based on the underlying price movements of a single security, a basket of securities, an index, a commodity, a debt issuance, and/or a foreign currency. Many economic and market factors will affect the value of structured products, and such factors may offset or magnify each other. Risk factors may include interest rate levels, implied volatility, and time remaining to maturity. Other risks may apply. Please carefully review the disclosure document or offering memorandum before investing.

Taxation

Williams Asset Management does not provide legal or tax advice. You should consult a legal or tax professional regarding your individual situation.

Technical Analysis

A method of evaluating securities by analyzing statistics generated by market activity, such as past prices and volume. Technical analysts do not attempt to measure a security's intrinsic value, but instead use charts and other tools to identify patterns that can suggest future activity.

Appendices

Appendix 3-A

The Ideal Week in Retirement

WHEN YOU IMAGINE LIFE AFTER RETIREMENT, WHAT DO YOU SEE? Do you picture yourself on a beach somewhere, relaxing without a care in the world? Do you imagine yourself spending more time with your family? Perhaps you want to spend time volunteering or pursuing activities you didn't have time for while you were working?

No matter what you envision yourself doing, keep one thing in mind: There are 24 hours in a day, 7 days in a week, and 52 weeks in a year. That's a lot of time to fill. What will you do that will be as fulfilling as your job once was?

You may find it useful to start thinking about time management in retirement by completing this hypothetical schedule. It may help you gain some perspective on how you will occupy yourself during this next phase of your life.

	MORNING	AFTERNOON	EVENING
Sunday			
Monday			
Tuesday			
Wednesday			
Thursday			
Friday			
Saturday			

Appendix 3-B

Retirement Vision Questionnaire

MANY PEOPLE FIND IT EASY TO PICTURE THEIR RETIREMENT, A TIME when every day is a vacation day. This image may be true for you as well, but some people do not have a clear vision of what their retirement will be like.

The following questions will help to get you thinking about your future and create a vision for your retirement:

1. What would your ideal day be like?
2. Is that ideal a day you could imagine living every day?
3. How do you spend your leisure time now?
4. Can you/will you continue these same activities postretirement?
5. What interests do you have that you may not have had the time or opportunity to explore while still working?
6. Will incorporating these new interests/activities be one of your goals?
7. Do you have many friendships or people with whom you will socialize?
8. Do you have strong community involvement? Will this involvement be an outlet for you?

9. Will you want to downsize your residence as you age?

10. Will you consider relocation as you age (e.g., to a warmer climate or one closer to relatives/friends)?

11. Do you enjoy traveling? Do you want to increase your travel in retirement?

12. With the extra time afforded to you, will you want to go out to eat more often? Will you want to go to more movies, plays/ musicals, or other entertainment events?

13. Do you currently volunteer? Have you considered volunteer work?

14. How will you maintain your health and fitness in retirement? Will you work out at a health club or exercise at home? Do you want to take up fitness activities?

15. Can you conceive of a week without work? Does part-time work appeal to you?

16. Do you want to leave a legacy for your children or grandchildren?

17. Do you wish to leave an endowment to a charity or charities?

18. Do you have other legacy or charitable goals (e.g., having a wing of a building at your alma mater named after you)?

Budget

MONTHLY INCOME	CURRENT	RETIREMENT
Wages, salary, tips		
Cash dividends		
Interest received		
Social Security income		
Pension income		
Rents, royalties		
Other income		
TOTAL MONTHLY INCOME	$	$

FIXED MONTHLY EXPENSES	CURRENT	RETIREMENT
Mortgage payment or rent		
Second home mortgage		
Automobile note		
Personal loans		

Credit cards		
Life insurance		
Disability insurance		
Health insurance		
Long-term care insurance		
Homeowner's insurance		
Automobile insurance		
Umbrella liability insurance		
SUBTOTAL	$	$

FIXED MONTHLY EXPENSES	**CURRENT**	**RETIREMENT**
Subtotal carried forward	$	$
Federal income taxes		
State income taxes		
FICA		
Real estate taxes		
Other taxes		
Savings (regularly)		
Investments (regularly)		
Retirement plan contributions		
TOTAL FIXED EXPENSES	$	$

VARIABLE MONTHLY EXPENSES	CURRENT	RETIREMENT
Electricity		
Gas		
Telephone		
Water		
Cable TV		
Home repairs and maintenance		
Home improvements		
Food		
Clothing		
Laundry		
Child care		
Personal care		
Automobile gas and oil		
Automobile repairs, etc.		
SUBTOTAL	$	$

VARIABLE MONTHLY EXPENSES	CURRENT	RETIREMENT
Subtotal carried forward	$	$
Other transportation		
Education expenses		
Entertainment/dining		
Recreation/travel		
Club/association dues		
Hobbies		
Gifts/donations		

Unreimbursed medical and dental expenses		
Miscellaneous		
TOTAL VARIABLE EXPENSES	$	$

NET CASH FLOW	CURRENT	RETIREMENT
Total monthly income		
Total fixed expenses		
Total variable expenses		
DISCRETIONARY INCOME (Income – Expenses)	$	$

Appendix 6-A

Risk Tolerance

WHAT TYPE OF INVESTOR ARE YOU?

The answers provided on this score sheet will help give you an indication of which investment strategy may be appropriate for your current needs. Just circle the corresponding point value, and then use the calculation provided to give you your total. Match the total to the strategy listed at the end of the score sheet.

Examine the time frame for the investment you're planning to make, because it's important to consider how long your money can be invested.

1. In approximately how many years do you expect to need this money?

	Points
A. 2–3 years	20
B. 4–6 years	38
C. 7–10 years	50
D. 10+ years	69

2. Do you expect to withdraw more than one-third of the money in this account within seven years (i.e., for retirement income, home down payment, or college tuition)?

	Points
A. No	20
B. Yes, in 2–3 years	0
C. Yes, in 4–7 years	12

Examine how you've planned ahead, because it's important to consider how prepared you are for immediate needs.

3. Do you have an emergency fund (i.e., savings of at least six months' after-tax income)?

	Points
A. No, I do not have an emergency fund.	8
B. I have an emergency fund, but it's less than six months' after-tax income.	3
C. Yes, I have an adequate emergency fund.	0

4. If you expect to have other major expenses (such as college tuition, home down payment, home repairs, etc.), do you have a separate savings plan for these expenses?

	Points
A. Yes, I have a separate savings plan for these expenses.	0
B. I do not expect to have any such expenses.	1
C. I intend to withdraw a portion of this money for these expenses (and have answered question 2 accordingly).	3
D. I have no separate savings plan for these items at this time.	4

Examine your current financial situation, because it's important to consider how this new account fits into your total financial picture.

5. Approximately what portion of your total investable assets★ is designated for this goal?

	Points
A. Less than 25%	0
B. Between 25% and 50%	1
C. Between 51% and 75%	2
D. More than 75%	4

6. Which ONE of the following describes your expected future earnings over the next five years? (Assume inflation will average 4%.)

	Points
A. I expect my earnings increases to far outpace inflation (due to promotions, etc.).	0
B. I expect my earnings increases to stay somewhat ahead of inflation.	1
C. I expect my earnings increases to keep pace with inflation.	2
D. I expect my future earnings to decrease (due to retirement, part-time work, depressed industry, etc.).	4

7. Approximately what portion of your monthly take-home income(s) goes toward paying off debt other than home mortgage?

	Points
A. Less than 10%	0
B. Between 10% and 25%	1
C. Between 26% and 50%	2
D. More than 50%	6

8. How many dependents do you have? (Include children you continue to support, elderly parents, etc.)

	Points
A. None	0
B. 1	1
C. 2–3	2
D. More than 3	4

Investable assets include your emergency fund, this account, bank accounts, retirement assets, CDs, mutual funds, cash value of life insurance, stocks or bonds, investment real estate, and so on, but they DO NOT include your principal residence or vacation home.

Examine your attitudes toward investing, because it's important to consider how experienced you are with different investments and levels of risk.

9. Part 1. Have you ever invested in individual bonds or bond investment vehicles, aside from U.S. savings bonds?

                                                       Points

   A. No, and I would be uncomfortable with the risk if I did. 10

   B. No, but I would be comfortable with the risk if I did. 4

   C. Yes, but I was uncomfortable with the risk. 6

   D. Yes, and I felt comfortable with the risk. 0

10. Part 2. Have you ever invested in individual stocks or stock investment vehicles?

                                                       Points

   A. No, and I would be uncomfortable with the risk if I did. 8

   B. No, but I would be comfortable with the risk if I did. 3

   C. Yes, but I was uncomfortable with the risk. 5

   D. Yes, and I felt comfortable with the risk. 0

11. When thinking about your investments, where would you place yourself on the following scale in terms of your comfort level with risk/potential reward?

A	B	C	D	E	F	G	H
12 points	7 points	5 points	3 points	2 points	1 point	0 points	0 points
Less Risk/ Less Potential Returns	Less Risk/ Less Potential Returns	Less Risk/ Less Potential Returns	Moderate Risk with Max Potential	Moderate Risk with Max Potential	Maximum Potential Return Regardless of Risk	Maximum Potential Return Regardless of Risk	Maximum Potential Return Regardless of Risk

12. Which ONE of the following statements describes your feelings toward choosing an investment?

                                                       Points

   A. I would prefer to select investment options that have a low degree of risk (i.e., it is unlikely I will lose my original investment). 12

   B. I prefer to select a mix of investment options, with emphasis on those with a low degree of risk, and a small portion in others that have a higher degree of risk, which may yield greater returns. 9

C. I prefer to select a balanced mix of investment options, some that have a low degree of risk and others that have a higher degree of risk, which may yield greater returns. 5

D. I prefer to select an aggressive mix of investment options, some that have a low degree of risk, but with emphasis on others that have a higher degree of risk, which may yield greater returns.   1

E. I would only select investment options that have a higher degree of risk and a greater potential for higher returns. 0

13. If you could increase your chances of improving your returns by taking more risk, would you:

                                                     Points

A. Be willing to take a lot more risk with all your money? 0
B. Be willing to take a little more risk with all your money? 3
C. Be willing to take a little more risk with some of your money? 6
D. Be unlikely to take much more risk? 10

Score and Strategy

Use the following calculation to determine your point score and identify the appropriate strategy listed below.

A. Add your points for questions 1–2. _____

B. Add your points for questions 3–12. _____

C. Subtract B from A. _____ (total points)

Strategy/Asset Class Mix	Points
Primarily Fixed Income: 75% Fixed Income; 25% Equity	0–9
Balanced Fixed Income-Oriented: 55% Fixed Income; 45% Equity	10–19
Balanced Equity-Oriented: 40% Fixed Income; 60% Equity	20–49
Primarily Equity: *20% Fixed Income; 80% Equity	50–69
Equity: 98% Equity; 2% Cash	70 or greater

Given your specific circumstances, if you believe that any of these strategies will be more suitable than the diversified strategy specified by the worksheet, you should consult your advisor to discuss the alternatives and make an appropriate recommendation.

*If your score points you to the growth strategy, consider investing in the aggressive strategy if the amount that you are investing for this goal represents only the aggressive portion of your total portfolio and if you already own more conservative investments—such as fixed-income and short-term securities—that can provide a balance to the short term.

Appendix 6-B

Standard Normal Distribution

STANDARD NORMAL DISTRIBUTION: Table Values Represent AREA to the LEFT of the Z score.

Z	.00	.01	.02	.03	.04	.05	.06	.07	.08	.09
-3.9	.00005	.00005	.00004	.00004	.00004	.00004	.00004	.00004	.00003	.00003
-3.8	.00007	.00007	.00007	.00006	.00006	.00006	.00006	.00005	.00005	.00005
-3.7	.00011	.00010	.00010	.00010	.00009	.00009	.00008	.00008	.00008	.00008
-3.6	.00016	.00015	.00015	.00014	.00014	.00013	.00013	.00012	.00012	.00011
-3.5	.00023	.00022	.00022	.00021	.00020	.00019	.00019	.00018	.00017	.00017
-3.4	.00034	.00032	.00031	.00030	.00029	.00028	.00027	.00026	.00025	.00024
-3.3	.00048	.00047	.00045	.00043	.00042	.00040	.00039	.00038	.00036	.00035
-3.2	.00069	.00066	.00064	.00062	.00060	.00058	.00056	.00054	.00052	.00050
-3.1	.00097	.00094	.00090	.00087	.00084	.00082	.00079	.00076	.00074	.00071
-3.0	.00135	.00131	.00126	.00122	.00118	.00114	.00111	.00107	.00104	.00100
-2.9	.00187	.00181	.00175	.00169	.00164	.00159	.00154	.00149	.00144	.00139
-2.8	.00256	.00248	.00240	.00233	.00226	.00219	.00212	.00205	.00199	.00193
-2.7	.00347	.00336	.00326	.00317	.00307	.00298	.00289	.00280	.00272	.00264
-2.6	.00466	.00453	.00440	.00427	.00415	.00402	.00391	.00379	.00368	.00357
-2.5	.00621	.00604	.00587	.00570	.00554	.00539	.00523	.00508	.00494	.00480
-2.4	.00820	.00798	.00776	.00755	.00734	.00714	.00695	.00676	.00657	.00639
-2.3	.01072	.01044	.01017	.00990	.00964	.00939	.00914	.00889	.00866	.00842
-2.2	.01390	.01355	.01321	.01287	.01255	.01222	.01191	.01160	.01130	.01101
-2.1	.01786	.01743	.01700	.01659	.01618	.01578	.01539	.01500	.01463	.01426
-2.0	.02275	.02222	.02169	.02118	.02068	.02018	.01970	.01923	.01876	.01831
-1.9	.02872	.02807	.02743	.02680	.02619	.02559	.02500	.02442	.02385	.02330
-1.8	.03593	.03515	.03438	.03362	.03288	.03216	.03144	.03074	.03005	.02938
-1.7	.04457	.04363	.04272	.04182	.04093	.04006	.03920	.03836	.03754	.03673
-1.6	.05480	.05370	.05262	.05155	.05050	.04947	.04846	.04746	.04648	.04551
-1.5	.06681	.06552	.06426	.06301	.06178	.06057	.05938	.05821	.05705	.05592
-1.4	.08076	.07927	.07780	.07636	.07493	.07353	.07215	.07078	.06944	.06811
-1.3	.09680	.09510	.09342	.09176	.09012	.08851	.08691	.08534	.08379	.08226
-1.2	.11507	.11314	.11123	.10935	.10749	.10565	.10383	.10204	.10027	.09853
-1.1	.13567	.13350	.13136	.12924	.12714	.12507	.12302	.12100	.11900	.11702
-1.0	.15866	.15625	.15386	.15151	.14917	.14686	.14457	.14231	.14007	.13786
-0.9	.18406	.18141	.17879	.17619	.17361	.17106	.16853	.16602	.16354	.16109
-0.8	.21186	.20897	.20611	.20327	.20045	.19766	.19489	.19215	.18943	.18673
-0.7	.24196	.23885	.23576	.23270	.22965	.22663	.22363	.22065	.21770	.21476
-0.6	.27425	.27093	.26763	.26435	.26109	.25785	.25463	.25143	.24825	.24510
-0.5	.30854	.30503	.30153	.29806	.29460	.29116	.28774	.28434	.28096	.27760
-0.4	.34458	.34090	.33724	.33360	.32997	.32636	.32276	.31918	.31561	.31207
-0.3	.38209	.37828	.37448	.37070	.36693	.36317	.35942	.35569	.35197	.34827
-0.2	.42074	.41683	.41294	.40905	.40517	.40129	.39743	.39358	.38974	.38591
-0.1	.46017	.45620	.45224	.44828	.44433	.44038	.43644	.43251	.42858	.42465
-0.0	.50000	.49601	.49202	.48803	.48405	.48006	.47608	.47210	.46812	.46414

STANDARD NORMAL DISTRIBUTION: Table Values Represent AREA to the LEFT of the Z score.

Z	.00	.01	.02	.03	.04	.05	.06	.07	.08	.09
0.0	.50000	.50399	.50798	.51197	.51595	.51994	.52392	.52790	.53188	.53586
0.1	.53983	.54380	.54776	.55172	.55567	.55962	.56356	.56749	.57142	.57535
0.2	.57926	.58317	.58706	.59095	.59483	.59871	.60257	.60642	.61026	.61409
0.3	.61791	.62172	.62552	.62930	.63307	.63683	.64058	.64431	.64803	.65173
0.4	.65542	.65910	.66276	.66640	.67003	.67364	.67724	.68082	.68439	.68793
0.5	.69146	.69497	.69847	.70194	.70540	.70884	.71226	.71566	.71904	.72240
0.6	.72575	.72907	.73237	.73565	.73891	.74215	.74537	.74857	.75175	.75490
0.7	.75804	.76115	.76424	.76730	.77035	.77337	.77637	.77935	.78230	.78524
0.8	.78814	.79103	.79389	.79673	.79955	.80234	.80511	.80785	.81057	.81327
0.9	.81594	.81859	.82121	.82381	.82639	.82894	.83147	.83398	.83646	.83891
1.0	.84134	.84375	.84614	.84849	.85083	.85314	.85543	.85769	.85993	.86214
1.1	.86433	.86650	.86864	.87076	.87286	.87493	.87698	.87900	.88100	.88298
1.2	.88493	.88686	.88877	.89065	.89251	.89435	.89617	.89796	.89973	.90147
1.3	.90320	.90490	.90658	.90824	.90988	.91149	.91309	.91466	.91621	.91774
1.4	.91924	.92073	.92220	.92364	.92507	.92647	.92785	.92922	.93056	.93189
1.5	.93319	.93448	.93574	.93699	.93822	.93943	.94062	.94179	.94295	.94408
1.6	.94520	.94630	.94738	.94845	.94950	.95053	.95154	.95254	.95352	.95449
1.7	.95543	.95637	.95728	.95818	.95907	.95994	.96080	.96164	.96246	.96327
1.8	.96407	.96485	.96562	.96638	.96712	.96784	.96856	.96926	.96995	.97062
1.9	.97128	.97193	.97257	.97320	.97381	.97441	.97500	.97558	.97615	.97670
2.0	.97725	.97778	.97831	.97882	.97932	.97982	.98030	.98077	.98124	.98169
2.1	.98214	.98257	.98300	.98341	.98382	.98422	.98461	.98500	.98537	.98574
2.2	.98610	.98645	.98679	.98713	.98745	.98778	.98809	.98840	.98870	.98899
2.3	.98928	.98956	.98983	.99010	.99036	.99061	.99086	.99111	.99134	.99158
2.4	.99180	.99202	.99224	.99245	.99266	.99286	.99305	.99324	.99343	.99361
2.5	.99379	.99396	.99413	.99430	.99446	.99461	.99477	.99492	.99506	.99520
2.6	.99534	.99547	.99560	.99573	.99585	.99598	.99609	.99621	.99632	.99643
2.7	.99653	.99664	.99674	.99683	.99693	.99702	.99711	.99720	.99728	.99736
2.8	.99744	.99752	.99760	.99767	.99774	.99781	.99788	.99795	.99801	.99807
2.9	.99813	.99819	.99825	.99831	.99836	.99841	.99846	.99851	.99856	.99861
3.0	.99865	.99869	.99874	.99878	.99882	.99886	.99889	.99893	.99896	.99900
3.1	.99903	.99906	.99910	.99913	.99916	.99918	.99921	.99924	.99926	.99929
3.2	.99931	.99934	.99936	.99938	.99940	.99942	.99944	.99946	.99948	.99950
3.3	.99952	.99953	.99955	.99957	.99958	.99960	.99961	.99962	.99964	.99965
3.4	.99966	.99968	.99969	.99970	.99971	.99972	.99973	.99974	.99975	.99976
3.5	.99977	.99978	.99978	.99979	.99980	.99981	.99981	.99982	.99983	.99983
3.6	.99984	.99985	.99985	.99986	.99986	.99987	.99987	.99988	.99988	.99989
3.7	.99989	.99990	.99990	.99990	.99991	.99991	.99992	.99992	.99992	.99992
3.8	.99993	.99993	.99993	.99994	.99994	.99994	.99994	.99995	.99995	.99995
3.9	.99995	.99995	.99996	.99996	.99996	.99996	.99996	.99996	.99997	.99997

Source: http://www.stat.tamu.edu/~lzhou/stat302/standardnormaltable.pdf,
Department of Statistics, College of Science, Texas A&M University.

Resources

CHAPTER 3

101 Secrets for a Great Retirement by Mary Helen Smith and Shuford Smith. Lowell House, 2000.

ReFirement: A Boomer's Guide to Life After 50 by James V. Gambone, PhD. Kirk House Publishers, 2000.

The New Retirementality by Mitch Anthony. Dearborn Trade, 2001.

CHAPTER 4

www.legacyit.com

www.yourafterlife.com

www.LifeBio.com

www.YourEthicalWill.com

www.FamilyStarProductions.com

www.HeritagePlanning.org

www.ExecutorsResource.com

www.WhatMattersBook.com

Cameron Thornton and Rodney Zeeb, *What Matters: A Novel* (Denver, CO: Sporting Culture Press, 2013). This story tells of a dying man who documents his values to ensure that his legacy beyond money is preserved. Visit www.whatmattersbook.com to learn more.

With Gratitude

THANK YOU FOR PURCHASING MY BOOK, *THE ART OF RETIREMENT*. I am pleased to tell you that 100 percent of the profits from the book are being donated to charitable organizations that I respect and want to help. I am grateful that your investment in my book will help the following charities continue to do their extraordinary work.

33% to Brigance Brigade

33% to Augie's Quest

17% to Maryland SPCA

17% to The Y of Central Maryland (to help disadvantaged youth attend summer camp)

THE BRIGANCE BRIGADE FOUNDATION

Amyotrophic lateral sclerosis (ALS), also known as Lou Gehrig's Disease, is a progressive neurodegenerative disease that affects motor nerve cells. These motor neurons carry impulses from the brainstem and spinal cord to the muscles. With ALS, a gradual degeneration of these cells occurs and eventually the muscles weaken and waste away (atrophy). Over time, people living with ALS lose the ability to walk, speak, eat, swallow, and breathe. Life expectancy is typically two to five years and the cost of living with ALS can be $250,000 or more annually.

In 2008, O.J. and his wife, Chanda, created the Brigance Brigade Foundation. The mission of the Brigance Brigade Foundation is to engage, encourage, and empower people living with ALS to live life through the provision of much-needed equipment, resource guidance, and support services as well as funding various ALS research initiatives. The Foundation coordinates with individuals and other ALS organizations to be sure those living with ALS are living a quality life. This support includes offering resource information, medical equipment, communication devices, and much more. Their support system fills the gaps where insurance, governmental programs, and other organizations cannot help.

To find out more about the Brigance Brigade Foundation or to make a donation, please visit www.BriganceBrigade.org.

O.J. Brigance

Photo courtesy of Phil Hoffmann,
Team Photographer, Baltimore Ravens

BRIGANCE
BRIGADE

AUGIE'S QUEST

Augie's Quest, the Muscular Dystrophy Association's ALS research initiative, is an aggressive, cure-driven effort focused on finding treatments and cures for ALS, or Lou Gehrig's disease.

Donations can be made on their website, www.augiesquest.org or mailed to:

Augie's Quest headquarters
9990 Mesa Rim Road, #100
San Diego, CA 92121

MARYLAND SPCA

The Maryland SPCA (http://www .mdspca.org) is one of the nation's oldest animal welfare organizations, founded in 1869 by a group of Baltimore citizens concerned about the welfare of the City's work horses. For years the Mary-

Helping Animals Since 1869

land SPCA provided water and emergency care and investigated complaints about horses that were used to pull wagons in daily commerce. In the 20th century, as the use of horses in commerce declined, the Maryland SPCA began to aid the City's homeless dogs. In the 1950s, they expanded their services to aid cats. In the early 1970s, they built a new kennel facility on the property, providing additional space and better facilities for the dogs and cats. In the mid-1990s, the Maryland SPCA began interviewing prospective adopters to make the best possible match between animal and home. In 1997, they renovated their kennels and added office space for adoptions. Today, the Maryland SPCA is one of the busiest adoption centers in the area, placing more than 3,000 pets a year into new homes.

Additional donations: Online donations can be made through their secure server by clicking the Donate Today button (http://www .mdspca.org/waystohelp/donate.html). Or you can mail your contribution to: Maryland SPCA, Development Office, 3300 Falls Road, Baltimore, MD 21211, or call (410) 235-8826, ext. 135, to make a credit card gift over the phone.

THE Y OF CENTRAL MARYLAND

Their Mission:

The Y of Central Maryland is a charitable organization dedicated to developing the full potential of every individual through programs that build healthy spirit, mind and body for all.

The Y of Central Maryland (www .ymaryland.org) has been serving the needs of the community for nearly 160 years.

Their Focus:

YOUTH DEVELOPMENT: Nurturing the potential of every child and teen.

HEALTHY LIVING: Improving Central Maryland's health and well-being.

SOCIAL RESPONSIBILITY: Giving back and providing support to our neighbors.

Their Vision:

Reaching over 240,000 people, the Y will be a primary catalyst for Central Maryland's families and individuals to achieve their full potential in spirit, mind and body.

Their Impact:

The Y is, and always will be, dedicated to developing healthy, confident, connected and secure children, adults, families and communities.

To make an additional donation, please visit http://ymaryland.org/giving-back

The Y of Central Maryland, 303 West Chesapeake Avenue, Towson, Maryland 21204, phone (443) 322-9622.

It's deeper here.

Acknowledgments

Ron Surz, President, PPCA; his insight of financial markets was a guiding source of knowledge.

Sydney LeBlanc, President, S. LeBlanc & Company; I couldn't have completed this project without her. She gave me confidence to write. She started out as my editor but became my good friend.

Jonathan Belanger, Sr. Investment Research Analyst, Commonwealth Financial Network (and talented musician); his thorough proofreading and feedback were appreciated more than my words on this paper can indicate. When I needed guidance, he was there for me.

Brian McCormick, Investment Research Analyst, Commonwealth Financial Network; he was able to turn data into a chart and made my points come alive on the pages.

Lincoln Webber, Sr. Real Assets Analyst, Commonwealth Financial Network; I could always count on Lincoln to confirm my data; a wealth of information.

Jim McGill, Retired Senior VP Finance and Administration, Johns Hopkins University; source of terrific, no-nonsense feedback.

Scott Rosenthal, CPA; he provided me with guidance on tax-related points.

Kol Birke, Director of Technology Product Evolution & Financial Behavior Specialist, Commonwealth Financial Network; even though he was busy planning his wedding, he always had time for me and this project. His knowledge of behavioral was essential.

Mark Atkinson, Director of Financial Planning and Head Trader, loyal and faithful employee of Williams Asset Management; was always there to proofread and give honest feedback.

Lisa Cutuli, VP, Altegris Investments; I could always count on Lisa to help me find data supporting my research.

Gina Grandone, Supervisor, Advisor Marketing–Communications– Corporate Marketing, Commonwealth Financial Network; was always there to help me make my charts look perfect.

Mark Colgan, CFP®, nationally recognized legacy planning expert and president of Plan Your Legacy; Mark shared his wisdom of ethical wills and why they are so important but also underutilized.

Nicole LaMoureux, Director, Advisor Marketing & Marketing Project Management–Communications–Corporate Marketing, Commonwealth Financial Network; was also a tremendous help in making my graphics look perfect.

Tere D'Amato, Vice President, Advanced Planning, Commonwealth Financial Network; her vast knowledge of Social Security is invaluable.

Stanley Max, M.L.S., Ph.D. (history), M.B.A., M.S. (statistics), Adjunct faculty, Department of Mathematics, Towson University; Stanley provided me with a refresher on statistics and use of the z table.

About the Author

Gary Williams is the president of Williams Asset Management in Columbia, Maryland. As of 2013 and with more than 19 years' experience, Mr. Williams has earned numerous credentials and designations, including:

CERTIFIED FINANCIAL
    PLANNER™ practitioner (1997)
Chartered Retirement Planning
    Counselor^SM (2004)
Accredited Investment Fiduciary® (2009)

*Gary S. Williams,
CFP®, CRPC®, AIF®*

Mr. Williams graduated from Towson University with a B.S. in Business Management and a concentration in Finance. He participates in industry-related membership organizations, including the Financial Planning Association and Baltimore Estate Planning Council.

As an active member of the community, Mr. Williams serves as a board member of the Dancel Family Y in Howard County and the Governance and Nominating Committee of Central Maryland Y's Board of Directors. Mr. Williams is a passionate supporter and is com-

mitted to ALS-related fundraising activities for research and equipment; to that end, he currently serves as an active board member of the
Brigance Brigade Foundation.

Contact Information:

Gary S. Williams
Williams Asset Management
8850 Columbia 100 Parkway, Suite 204
Columbia, MD 21045
Phone: (410) 740-0220
Email: Gary@WilliamsAsset.com

Disclosure: Securities and Advisory Services offered through Com-
monwealth Financial Network, member FINRA/SIPC, a Registered
Investment Adviser. Fixed insurance products and services offered by
Williams Asset Management.